i came upon a lighthouse

Praise for *I Came Upon a Lighthouse*

'Shantanu has given the world a real treat – by showing readers the most endearing side of a man who is seen as a superhero by millions.'

– Shobhaa De

'A unique, trans-cultural, age-obliterating friendship between a millennial and a multinational business icon.'

– Bachi Karkaria

'A 27-year-old whose friendship with industrialist-philanthropist Ratan Tata began over a shared love for strays revisits the extraordinary story in this new illustrated book.'

– *Mid Day*

'A millennial's tribute to his octogenarian friend with whom he shares a love for homeless dogs ... a very charming book.'

– Pritish Nandy

'The book can serve as a guide for those who want to know lesser-known facts about the doyen of Indian industry. One gets to know a side of Tata that's goofy and witty.'

– *The Tribune*

'A riveting, easy, effortless and very gentle and lovely read ... a close-up view of one of India's most revered public figures living today.'

– Freddy Birdy

i came upon a lighthouse

a short memoir of life with
RATAN TATA

SHANTANU NAIDU

illustrated by SANJANA DESAI

HarperCollins *Publishers* India

First published in India in hardback in 2021 by
HarperCollins *Publishers*

First published in India in paperback by HarperCollins *Publishers* 2022
4th Floor, Tower A, Building No. 10, Phase II, DLF Cyber City,
Gurugram, Haryana – 122002
www.harpercollins.co.in

8 10 9 7

P-ISBN: 978-93-5489-741-2
E-ISBN: 978-93-9032-753-9

Cover illustration: Sanjana Desai
Cover design: Amit Malhotra
Book layout and design: Isha Nagar

Printed and bound at
Replika Press Pvt. Ltd.

MIX
Paper | Supporting responsible forestry
FSC™ C016779

This book is produced from independently certified FSC® paper to ensure responsible forest management.

Dedicated to my friend and saviour,
my dog Winter

Contents

A Note by Ratan Tata

A SHARED CONCERN FOR the welfare of the homeless, hungry, ill-treated and abandoned dogs and cats brought Shantanu and me together. He and his young friends had been bootstrapping a small start-up in Pune to feed, care for and find homes for these poor animals. He earned recognition when they made reflective collars, based solely on passion and kindness for animals.

Knowing my love for dogs, he wrote to my office, not even expecting a response. I was impressed by what they had done and the compassion that Shantanu and the college kids had shown by investing their personal time and resources. I decided to invest in his start-up, and they received not just support but also encouragement to grow it through personal involvement.

I was also impressed by his sincerity and offered him a job on the completion of his studies. Shantanu took the job and joined me in my office. He shares time between assisting me in our philanthropic activities, the development of the Tata Trusts' long-term plans and helping with start-up investments. He has become a member of the small team which is driven by their desire to help others. Each day has a lesson to be learnt and each day is one of fulfilment that he has brought happiness to someone, or sadness at not having been able to do so.

I hope Shantanu can be a shining light of kindness who will continue to be driven by genuine goodwill, and I am thankful that he is able to help others from deep within his heart.

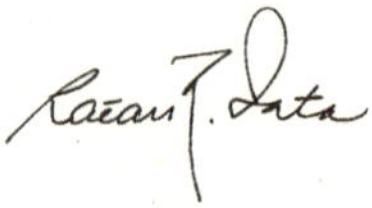

Ratan Tata
December 2020

Introduction

THE PAGES OF THIS book are the result more of heart and story and less of artistic capability. It is my honest narration of what some of you might see as adventures, others as essays, and even more of you as a running journal, and all of you would be right.

Many of you will turn these pages to know about Mr Ratan Tata. And while I wish I could have done only that—to fully understand him from how I see him—this is a short memoir of my life where it overlaps his.

It took courage to bring these stories to you. To be able to put my life out there, to be seen and be vulnerable. But the purpose of writing them was to bring to you facets of someone who grew into so many roles: mentor, friend, a warm-hearted and wise guide. Facets unknown to the world that has revered him only as a beloved industrialist.

On the day he finished reading the manuscript, he wrote me a letter to say how touched he was to see these stories on paper. It is a letter I hold dear, especially for the lines where he also wrote about Mr J.R.D. Tata. 'Jeh [as JRD was often called] used to enjoy embarrassing me, but it was our mutual love and affection for each other that grew exponentially. You have many attributes that I admire. You are like a son or younger brother, I enjoy being in your company.'

My only hope for you is for these pages to leave your heart a little fuller, slightly richer, and to share what I have seen, just as I saw it.

As a celebration of the circumstances that brought us together, all author proceeds from this book will be used for the welfare of animals in need. For this, I thank you with all my heart.

1

Motopaws

STORIES THAT END pleasantly don't always start in pleasant places. This one certainly doesn't. It's hard to forget the late night when my motorcycle screeched to a stop under one of the many orange streetlights on a road in Pune. Cars sped by threateningly. I knew what I had seen that had made me pull over. Falsely hoping it might be something else, I looked at the centre of the road in the distance. A white dog with brown spots lay in a pool of his own blood.

I was right the first time.

This is where it started—the first nudge of destiny's curious finger on the first domino.

He wasn't run over just once. And it wasn't even a one-off incident. It was the sixth time I had had to pull over in those couple of months with nothing left to do but stare helplessly. I used to imagine doing terrible things to the people who had run over the dogs—worse to those who had run them over after they had died. Grief would fill my insides thinking about their last moments and how lonely they must have been, apart from their obvious pain. Were they crossing the road to meet their friend? To see their puppies? To find food? But it's not like my conscience spared me any shame. I should have had, at the very least, the decency to move the dead dog to the sidewalk. I didn't.

At work the next day, with colourful curses, I would go on to describe how evil we are as a race, not letting anyone do their job until my passionate preaching was done. On one such preachy morning, a colleague pulled me aside hesitantly to tell me about the time he had run a dog over several years ago.

'I had no choice. It was either that or to swerve the car at the last minute and drive my family off the road,' he said.

'Last minute?'

'Yes, last minute. I didn't see him until the very last minute.'

After making sure I didn't hold it against him and that we were still friends, he left. But the 'last minute' part of the story stayed with me. Was this happening with all the drivers that ran over dogs? Over the next few weeks, I was obsessed with finding out and set out to speak to people who had been in accidents involving dogs or close calls of some sort. All of them had a similar story to tell.

'They appear so suddenly.'

'The streets aren't well lit.'

'I didn't even get a chance to slow down ...'

If there was any way of fixing this, it wasn't just about making the dogs visible. They had to be visible from a distance. Enough distance to give a driver time to think about what his next move should be to avoid the dog on the road.

I took all of this and sat down with Mihira, the girl I was seeing then. To call Mihira an animal lover would be a grossly unfair understatement. She was a cute little passionately dedicated animal soldier who would go to great lengths for a rescue. We discussed making the dogs visible.

'We should put something bright on them. Shiny collars!'

I can imagine how very lame that must sound now. Mihira must have really been into me to be into this. Or equally lame.

But being her sweet, unselfish self, she obliged.

'What would we make them from?'

'Well, we don't have a lot of money, so something cheap? My fashion designer friends said we could use denims.'

'Yes! Oh, oh! We can cut denim pants! Let me go home and stitch one.'

Cut pants and make dogs shine. Sure.

As an automotive design engineer at Tata Elxsi, I was aware of the reflective tape used on cars. It's bright, is seen from a distance and reflects any light that falls on it at a direct angle. I bought a few meters of the red tape for Mihira and she brought back a stitched collar the very next day, done well enough to get us excited. She also put slits and a button on it.

'Let's test this! Let's collar a dog.'

Growing up in Pune you get to know pretty much all the nooks and crannies of the city. We went to a rather lazy one where a dog was kind enough to let us put the collar on. In fact, he didn't care as long as he was being cuddled. With his wiggly butt and happy with this sudden attention, he didn't even notice us putting it on. We took a ride around the block and returned with the headlight on.

Words cannot capture the glory with which the clueless dog shone that night. A beautiful, glowing phoenix! A fat and cuddly phoenix that couldn't fly. But the collar worked!

As with any project you are giddy with excitement about, we decided to name it first. A weird christening process later, 'Motopaws' was finalized. 'Moto' for the drivers and 'paws' for the dogs. Concerns were raised about it sounding very similar to 'menopause', but we stuck with it anyway. A local tailor was willing to cut up denims and stitch us 500 collars. I don't know if it was because of the ridiculousness of Motopaws or because of the fact that it involved dogs, but the rest of the team just put itself together. Mihira, my best friend Sukrut and I, with the addition of another friend called Kalyani, branched out to discover hyper, young students dying to join this ... well, for the time being, let's call it 'charade'. All of them donated denims they were no longer using. Large, small, ripped, pink, purple ones even. Denims that we dumped on the no-longer-enthusiastic tailor.

The launch was planned with the maximum extravagance that our small group of students could allow. The logo. The name. Practicality nauseates me, I say proudly, even as it has bitten me in the rear often.

'This has never happened before; we really need to get the city's attention.'

'Okay, what do you suggest?'

See, the thing about this team of fifteen-odd youngsters was that it could be rallied to do anything, absolutely anything, as long as I demonstrated conviction in whatever we were about to do. We partnered with Harley Davidson, Triumph Motorcycles and KTM motorcycles to do the launch with us. Their intimidatingly cool-looking riders promised to join us across the city to collar the dogs on launch day.

Each night closer to the launch was sleepless and thrilling.

The big day showed up rather suddenly. Volunteers were in proper uniform. Motorcycles rumbled out one after another to their assigned dog-collaring areas. Goosebumps of every variety.

Everyone had put faith in a twenty-three-year-old skinny me. And I couldn't understand why. If I saw me, I would probably roll my eyes and walk away. But for whatever reason, they showed up.

I owed this much. To the dogs lying in pools of blood with nobody by their side in their final moments. The puppies

who would never understand what happened to their mothers. The few who had risked their lives and swerved at the last minute to save dog lives. And everyone who showed up that day.

We had 500 collars and we collared 500 dogs. So many more could have been collared, but we only had so much money. And then, we waited.

I woke up to someone sharing a link to the first article that was published. Before I finished reading it, there was another. And it went on. Not long after, all the large online media houses were obsessing over Motopaws. At one point, we didn't even know where it was getting featured nor did we have any control over it. A scandal could not have gotten more attention that day. But it is obvious why. I mean, nobody thought a bunch of students would just go out and fill the night streets with shiny dogs.

But the most important responses, the ones we were looking for, were the anonymous comments online, in the corners of the internet, from people who had spotted the collared dogs in the night, or on a blind kerb, or when speeding down an empty street.

'Where did these come from?'

'Whoever did this, thank you!'

'Guys, I just saw the craziest thing last night ...'

'I could slow down just in time.'

'I was speeding home from my night shift but ...'

Every morning, Naina (as I call my father in Telugu) phoned from work to check which newspapers had featured us. Every evening, he returned with the print copy and put it in a file. The file grew very fat very quickly.

'I am sure Mr Tata would like to know about Motopaws. He likes dogs,' Naina mentioned in a suspiciously nonchalant way one day.

'Yes, I think he does,' I replied, based on whatever little I knew of Mr Tata's interests.

But I humoured him: 'Do you have his email?'

'No, but I could ask around.'

I didn't know if he forgot, but after some very cursory internet searches, I surely did. Not because reaching out to him successfully was insignificant, but because it was too significant a thing, and I couldn't comprehend it happening.

Everyone looks up to the house of Tatas. Everyone dreams of meeting him. Every other Indian. What was so different about me? There must be a sea of phenomenal minds more deserving of an audience with him. I was a speck.

My family didn't just look up to him like every other person familiar with the phrase 'Tata–Birla'. We worshipped the Tatas as a foundational part of our family history.

My great-grandfather worked for Tata Power. My grandfather for Tata Electrical. Naina for Tata Motors. My cousin for Tata Consultancy. And then me for Tata Elxsi, making me the fifth generation in the Tata Group.

No, we had never met or interacted with any of the Tatas. None of us had been Tata executives either. The Tata history has no mention of us Naidus. We worked in whatever roles we were found deserving of, largely just engineers, and we were proud of that heritage. My great-grandmother (now ninety) has a silver embossed coin featuring Jamshedji Tata in the house shrine, next to a picture of him before which she lights incense sticks every evening, alongside idols of seven different gods and a naked baby picture of me that remains there despite repeated protests. She believes the Tatas are god-sent world-fixers. I would be lying if I said the rest of the family didn't feel the same way.

So, no, I refused to believe I would see Mr Tata. I chose self-doubt and self-deprecation instead. Until Naina sat me down one day with the big fat file of news clippings.

'Someone I know was part of the legal team at the Tata Trusts. Maybe we can send this with him?'

Like an emotional teenager, I spent a long time writing him a letter that ended with: 'Someday, I would very much like to see you, Mr Tata.' All that was missing was XOXO, hearts and hugs. It was hard not to mock my own audacity to even think the universe would oblige such a request. I attached the Tata newsletters talking about Motopaws and pictures of the young team.

With the letter carefully put in the file, and an introduction from Naina, I went to the lawyer. The second domino.

'If you could just give this to his office ...' I said, not even having the guts to add, 'to Mr Tata.'

He agreed to drop it off at his office the next time he went to Mumbai, but nothing more.

I was happy that I tried. If nothing happened now, it would be okay. The pain of wondering about the what-ifs is harsher than the pains of rejection. The next week the lawyer told me the file had been delivered.

If the hope of something actually coming out of this was described with the analogy of a fire (channelling my tragic inner poet here), it was the size of a huge forest fire the day he said it had been delivered. With passing weeks, it reduced to a bonfire, a fireplace fire, then a flickering lamp and, finally, a firefly's butt.

I told Naina to let it go. That the letter was probably lost in the many million things that are sent to him. Or that he couldn't possibly respond to something like this. Naina, however, had a resolve I simply could not understand. He spoke with confidence as if he were his childhood friend Ratan.

'He will reply. If he sees it, he will reply. He has not seen it yet.'

Weeks passed by. I was studying for the GMAT, the entrance exam for an MBA abroad. Naina had given me the option of becoming an industrial designer or doing an MBA and I chose the latter for its financial safety (there is no such thing). I was really into it.

We used to have this 'He will reply' and 'I don't think so' exchange every now and then during my study breaks, with the occasional variety of:

'He cares about everyone who writes to him.'

'Tatas don't ignore people.'

'Even if he doesn't meet you, he will write back.'

'The newspapers say he is in Germany now. Let him return, then you'll see.'

Two hundred miles away, at Mr Tata's office at the Elphinstone building in south Mumbai, the file was looked at by the girl at the front desk. She knew all such files went to a particular person in the office who had shown no particular interest in looking at things empathetically. But not this file. She held on to this one. She showed it to the other two women working there, and all three of them decided that it must be seen by Mr Tata himself. They protected it and waited. When Mr Tata returned, the file was on his desk. In the many dominoes on my journey to meeting Mr Tata, these three women were critical. The final domino.

Shortly after, there was a letter from Mumbai:

Dear Shantanu,

Thank you for your email and for the kind sentiments which you have expressed.

I am impressed by your dedicated efforts in successfully launching the innovative campaign 'Motopaws' and I am also pleased to know about the campaign 'Paws for a Cause'. Animal welfare is an area which I am very passionate about. It would be a pleasure meeting you for discussions on this subject. Please get in touch with my office for a suitable date for our meeting.

With regards and my best wishes in your endeavour,

Yours sincerely,

Ratan N. Tata

See, when a multi-generational Tata employee family receives a letter like this, the celebrations are nothing short of running naked in the streets. Here are a few things that were repeated multiple times in a very short span that day by the Naidu family, with the kind of giddiness that can only come from a childhood sugar rush.

'Did you see! He said he is IMPRESSED!! MR TATA is impressed with MY son!!!'

'HE SIGNED IT HIMSELF!!'

'You are going to meet A TATA!!!'

'Our ancestors would be so proud.'

The meeting was set for two months later, in September 2016. Those were not pleasant months. The Motopaws collars started cracking. The reflective tape we used was meant for cars and flat surfaces and not for stitching on denims. It couldn't handle the circular stresses. We researched deeper, and we researched thoroughly, and we finally replaced it with an industrial retro-reflective fabric that worked wonders and fixed the issue. To this day, we use the same material, despite the severe damage to our pockets, to ensure the quality and sustainability of Motopaws collars.

The meeting was drawing close, with only a couple of weeks to go. One monsoon evening, I was riding my motorcycle when it started to pour heavily. I decided not to pull over to wait out the storm and kept riding home. Suddenly, another rider emerged, completely blindsiding me. I hit the front brakes in panic, sending me into the road divider. The bike dragged me with it.

My leg wouldn't move. I was bleeding from more than one place. In the middle of the street, as the storm continued, I sat myself up, thinking of only one thing:

'How am I now going to see Mr Tata?'

2

A Promise Is a Promise

'HOW DARE YOU put your life in danger before meeting Mr Tata!'

All sorts of healing methods short of sacrifices for Greek gods were performed to make sure I could walk properly before seeing him. I was scared to even cough in the house.

'Do you want to cough in front of Mr Tata? Do you? What will he think!' Just Indian parent things, I guess.

All that was left was babyproofing the house till this meeting was done.

I decided to take Sukrut with me. He had been key in building Motopaws from the ground up. We decided to both wear white shirts to seem as professional as we possibly could and bought expensive ones for the meeting. It was also agreed that he would carry his family camera for taking two pictures only. No less and no more. I would take one of him with Mr Tata and he'd do the same for me. We did not wish to intrude but our moms and grannies had guns to our backs.

I didn't have time to be happy about all of this, really. That place in my mind was well occupied by anxiety. I remember thinking that nothing that came out of my mouth could possibly be of value in a meeting with Mr Ratan-freaking-Tata. Self-deprecation was always the winner.

We arrived a day early at the Hotel Astoria in Fort, Mumbai. Naina took us around to explore the different streets lined with monsoon-happy trees, to Marine Drive and the lanes packed with English buildings that were now occupied by big offices. It was my first visit to south Mumbai. Occasionally we would get stuck in the rain, but Naina used that time to introduce me to the city. I have warm memories of that day. Very rarely do I get to spend time like that with him. In my long-standing romance with Mumbai, I had only just begun to flirt. We walked around, pretending not to be nervous about the next morning, and for a few hours it worked, especially with Sukrut there.

The freaking beacon of happiness that he is, he can never be consumed with the mundane hurt, pain and worry that plague us all. Sukrut has no filters in life. Laughs at all the inappropriate times, in all the

inappropriate places. Very few things can dampen his spirit. Our friendship could easily be mistaken for a relationship, but are you really even best friends if people don't ask you that? God bless Sukrut.

The morning of the meeting, we dressed in silence. Naina ironed my shirt, since he had trust issues after my history of burning through several pieces of apparel on different important occasions. He walked us down to the beautiful Venetian-Gothic office building (I looked it up). The whole square was full of British-era buildings and the air hung heavy with stories I knew nothing about. Naina said he would wait downstairs.

I could see how much he wanted to meet him too. But there was no way he would even think of suggesting such a thing. He was too self-made and proud to ask to share his son's big moment. It broke my heart a little.

On the top floor, a tall, serious, bespectacled man, who I later found out was R. Venkataramanan, managing trustee of the Tata Trusts, looked at us. (Imagine Professor McGonagall, but male.)

'We have an appointment with Mr Tata,' I blurted.

He nodded and opened the door. 'This way.'

The girl at the front desk was Denese, warm in her welcome and kind in her smile. She escorted us to a couch where we sat down in a nervous huddle, too stressed to appreciate how delightfully charming she was, which was a topic filed away in our minds to be discussed later. Then, we waited.

I stared at the door of Mr Tata's cabin. There was a moment when someone went in to serve him coffee. As the door closed slowly, I caught a glimpse of him eating cookies in slow motion, and I elbowed Sukrut to see what I saw. I found myself wondering what kind of cookies Ratan Tata must eat. Would they be very different from what Amma bought for me? Only moments later, he came out to get us.

Smart in his white check shirt and welcoming smile, his presence was overwhelming.

Pointing at the bandage on my hand, he asked with a tongue-in-cheek smile:

'What happened, did a dog bite you?'

That nervous joke of his will forever be the very first words he said to me and I don't know whether to be happy or sad about it. But I've only grown to love his wit so much more every day.

'I'm sorry, that was a tasteless joke. And I'm sorry I kept you waiting. Please, come in,' he said, holding the door open.

His voice was deep and rumbly, yet rich with affection—which seemed to be a part of everything he did. The kindness in his eyes or the polite curve in his tone, as if we were owed something even when we weren't. It reminded me of Gandalf.

We showed him the Motopaws journey. He kept repeating how innovative he believed the idea was. Incapable of handling praise, we continued to smile sheepishly, with an occasional 'Oh, stop it, you' chuckle escaping. We showed him the music video we had made about the story of a stray puppy named Johnny whose mother had been run over, leaving him to fend for himself.

'I hope you haven't shown a dog getting run over, I couldn't bear to see that.'

We assured him there was nothing traumatizing in there. How can someone be a wise owl and so soft-hearted at the same time, I still wonder.

He put on the headphones and watched the whole video patiently, and for those entire three minutes we stared at him.

Looking at him, a sense of calm took over. Everything bad just washed away. His presence was all-encompassing. His features seemed so ... unique. His sturdy Parsi nose, the silver hair at the front, clean and wavy across the forehead. A comforting breeze—that's how I would describe him. The kind that carries happy memories and makes you think about life in a good way. Enough cannot be said about the grace with which he acted and spoke. Everything he did was soft and polite.

He finished the video and said, 'I am so touched by the

sensitivity you have towards these animals. I feel the exact same way, and I am happy you feel it too.'

Providential dispensation is such that nobody in life is ever completely happy. But in that moment, I was.

I could imagine my ancestors going nuts above. *Ancestors!* Naina had given me a print showing the five generations of the Naidu clan working for the Tatas lined up in a basic collage. I pulled it out with a chest that I now feel wasn't puffed up enough.

'I thank them for their service. I'm sorry I didn't know them.'

Then out of the blue came the question: 'Tell me, what can I do for you?'

I didn't like this turn in the conversation. We had decided not to ask for or accept any form of help. That was not why we were there.

'Nothing, Mr Tata. I came here to build a relationship, to help you materialize any vision that you might have for animals.'

He didn't seem to understand what I was trying to say and repeated the 'How can I help you' question several times in many indirect ways. But we repeatedly emphasized that we didn't have an ask. It was becoming less and less pleasant, diluting the intentions with which we were actually there.

I realized almost a year later that so many people go to him with empty hands only to return with them full. He must have come to believe nobody comes to him without an ask. (Not that it is wrong to have one or that it bothers him if they want something. He will treat them with just as much kindness, if not more, and I admire him for it.) But I didn't have one.

Eventually he put the matter aside, and like an ideal pet parent showed us pictures of his two dogs, Tito and Tango.

'Would you like to meet them?'

'We'd love to meet them.'

'Okay. I have one last meeting. Why don't I finish it and then you can come meet Tito and Tango?'

My forefathers' distant screams as they lost their minds and pulled out their angel hair were audible. (Yes, I have assumed they are in heaven.)

Very awkwardly, we requested a picture with the both of us. But for some reason it felt very ... wrong. I guess after having spent time with him, it felt like nothing else really mattered. But I had promised mother, grandmother, great-grandmother and her shrine with the naked baby picture.

'Of course you can take a picture.'

Sukrut pulled out the DSLR, as planned, and Mr Tata stared at it and remarked, 'Wow, that's a big camera.'

'Well, you are a big man,' said the not-so-subtle Sukrut.

The 'sanskari' boys that we were trying to be, we bent to touch his feet and seek his blessings on our way out, but he didn't let us. 'That's not okay,' he said, giving us each a paternal hug instead.

We waited on the same couch outside and saw Denese again. This time, we were too excited to appreciate how charming she was, and again it was to be discussed at a later date. He finished his meeting rather quickly, perhaps because we were waiting for him.

On our way out, he was kind enough to introduce us to his colleagues. Deepthi, a smart soldier with a pixie haircut, who I was a little scared of. Imagine Tinkerbell but with a hunting knife. And then there was Parizaad. The only way to ever see or talk to Mr Tata was through her, and it still is. She guards the gates of the chairman's office from unsolicited strangers trying to get to Mr Tata for not-so-worthy reasons. The mama bear of the chairman's office.

Standing there in the midst of Deepthi, Parizaad and Denese, the three ladies who had guarded the file I had sent, I could never have imagined the role they were to play in my life four years later, or how much I would come to love and adore them. Mr Tata wasn't the only blessing. He came with three more.

Coming out of the building, I looked for Naina. He saw Mr Tata and burst into an ear-to-ear grin. They shook hands semi-vigorously. Worlds collided. The person whose stories I had grown up listening to and the person who told me those stories were both facing each other. To the comfort of us all, Naina did not faint.

It was a short drive in Mr Tata's Range Rover that we were examining with googly eyes. The simple Colaba house had a big lawn that overlooked the ocean. Three chairs were pulled up and all of us were served lychee juice (which I loved and is still served at his place). He was so clearly a happier person then. The legal troubles of October around the leadership of the Tata Group had not arrived yet. His smiles were less tired. His eyes quite brighter. There wasn't a lot of talking. But his presence was hard to ignore and continued to envelop us through the dreamy, ocean-side Mumbai evening.

Tito and Tango were gorgeous giant babies with thick, lion-like fur coats. I was in one corner playing with Tito while Sukrut played with Tango. It was the perfect end to the day.

Sukrut asked him if he could get his camera out.

'You can do whatever you want,' he replied matter-of-factly, maintaining the kind tone, which by now I had realized was a natural part of him. Of all the pictures we took that evening, there was one of him playing with Tito that we framed and mailed him. It sits on his library mantle even today, and is featured in his second Instagram post.

I did not want to overstay my welcome. Okay, fine, I wanted to. But we took his leave, with him insisting on having the car drop us back at the Astoria Hotel.

Sukrut and I didn't say a word on the way back. We did not care about Motopaws at that time. We did not care about the pictures. We did not care about the fact that this was our first and probably last ride in his Range Rover. We even forgot to talk about Denese from the front desk. We were beyond all of this and everything seemed superficial now without him there. We had only met him that day, but his absence already felt like a void.

As I replayed the day and the time I had spent with him in my head, I suddenly distinctly remembered something that Mr Tata had said to Naina as we were leaving the office. It was a dictum I will never forget. With his large hand on Naina's tiny Naidu shoulder, in the most reassuring way possible:

'Don't worry, sir, I will take care of your son.'

Nobody had pushed him to say that. There was no prelude to this sentence. Naina hadn't made any request, nor had I. But for whatever reason, he felt he had to say that, and so he made that promise.

I cannot recount the number of times Mr Tata has gone above and beyond to keep this promise. He has been there when I have been in a rut. He has been there when I have celebrated. He has been there without me asking for it. He has been there when I might have been annoying. He has been there when I asked for his blessing to compile these stories!

In the pages that follow, there are many roles he plays. Sometimes a selfless friend, sometimes a protective brother, other times a guide with a stern hand on my shoulder. At twenty-seven, without the knowledge of how the rest of my life will pan out, I am happy to have found someone I can describe this way.

The universe may find me ungrateful for saying this, but I have been gifted a guardian—one I find it hard to believe I deserve.

A guardian probably nobody deserves, and yet a guardian to many.

3

Butter Soap

THE WHOLE ROOM was laughing at me. I didn't get up and leave because I didn't know if my legs would work. Nobody had ever made me feel so uncertain and insulted about anything.

It was the first day of my coaching class for the GMAT. A lot of money had been paid to put me in that room for the next six months. A lot at least by my family's standards. In the last few minutes of the class, Professor Ghosh was telling us about the one thing Indian students everywhere cock up their ears for:

'How do I get in?'

The question-and-answer session was abused to its limit.

'Which Ivy League is the best for finance placements?'

'How much do I need to score for the big three?'

'I saved a kid from a fire, started my own company, then sold it to Google and became a millionaire, but donated it all for children in need. Will I get into Harvard?'

All sorts of questions were flying in the room, questions I didn't even know the context of! The room was full of toxically motivated, competitive students who knew exactly what they wanted, and they were going to get it—no matter what.

'Any final questions?'

My itchy butt:

'What if I got into an Ivy League but wanted to come back to India?'

Silence turned to laughter. The kind that doesn't die down. Some ridicule I expected, but not this. The humiliation from that moment still follows me. I looked pleadingly to Professor Ghosh, who was smiling helplessly as everyone else continued to laugh.

'Why would you want to come back? Just stay here then,' someone said.

I could pay off a significant chunk of my student loan if I had a dollar every time I have been asked this over the years.

That birthed my obsession with this exam. Everyone I knew had already moved to the US for their masters, which today is a pretty typical trajectory for any Indian student and none of us can remember why. Post-its on every wall with tips, points to remember, formulae. I worked hard with Professor Ghosh: emails and messages back and forth and back again, full of queries and doubts. The study leave from the office was borderline dangerous. Night shifts at work were spent solving question banks. I had to get into an Ivy. Nothing else mattered. I don't know why I had to—if it was to redeem myself or to keep my promise to Naina or if it was truly what I wanted.

This obsession took me away from friends, and even from Mihira. With time her priorities changed, understandably. She started her master's in wildlife conservation in Pune. We broke up, but moving on synced with the rigorous exam prep. Come December, I gave the four-hour-long marathon of a GMAT. But I had choked—my fear had got the better of me.

The score was in the mid-600s. I was ashamed.

It didn't make any sense. I hadn't cut corners. It had to be my nerves. I had worked towards this for so long that the reality of getting to the exam hall completely threw me off. It just did not make sense. The denial that followed was toxic. After a week of self-pity and 'It's okay, we are here' sentiments from friends and family, I decided this wasn't how I wanted it to end. If it was in fact my incapability, it would show in the second attempt too. *Then* I could give up. I scheduled another exam for fifteen days later and spent the rest of December, including Christmas and New Year's Eve, diving deeper and fixing my nerves. After my second attempt on the first day of the year, I called father.

'Hello Naina, guess how much I got.'

'700?'

'Nope.'

'740??'

'Nope. 760! I got a 760!'

I have often seen, many times in my own life, instances where you may deserve something. But it doesn't always mean it'll be handed to you without an initial struggle, or at the time when you want it. I don't have a reason for why this happens, but I'd like to think it's a test of how badly you want something. I am sure many others who have scored this much or higher have done so matter-of-factly, without it being a big highlight of their lives. But I cannot pretend it wasn't. Something came to fruition that day and so it was special. It was a teary-eyed rickshaw ride back home, me alternating between laughs and sobs, scorecard clutched so tightly to my heart I almost had to request another one. I was one step farther from the laughing classroom.

All of the Ivy Leagues had already closed their applications or were in their last rounds, where international students were not encouraged to apply. The only two left were Harvard and Cornell.

It is common knowledge that Mr Tata has attended both schools. Undergrad at Cornell, and the Advanced Management Program at Harvard. I knew how competitive it was. Business school applications aren't just about the score. They're also about the story of how you got there. I had my Motopaws story. I had the 760 score. But a lot of candidates had a lot more things. I couldn't have conjured something rockstar-ish in a week's time, and I didn't want to. It wouldn't have been authentic. It wouldn't have been me. The only area to strengthen was the recommendations. We were allowed two and one was from my ex-supervisor. A second recommendation letter from someone respected who knew me well, someone like—I don't know—Mr Tata?

The thought felt obscene. So much energy was spent not asking him for anything. I had politely shied away from his donation offer to Motopaws after our first meeting, but one day a stern colleague of his called to tell me it wasn't okay to continue like this, and that Mr Tata felt bad that we students were digging deep in our pockets. (On several occasions since, I have seen him try to persistently help others whose work he appreciates and respects and, in a way, probably wishes he could do himself. And if he believes an initiative can grow and have a larger impact, he will absolutely try and help.) So I gave in and accepted. Motopaws went from just Motopaws to a 'Ratan Tata-backed start-up'. A title we did not chase, but one that has given us a foundation of trust nonetheless.

We used that money to scale up to eleven cities. There are now over fifteen independent Motopaws chapters across the country, three different production facilities, with international chapters in Nepal and Bangladesh. I tried to give him frequent updates about how Motopaws was spending the money, and about our quick growth and challenges. But eventually our conversations got more honest, more informal, and moved beyond Motopaws.

Strange was this world of Ivy Leagues. To be wanted by what have been accepted as the best institutions in the world is an intoxicating wish that only gets stronger as you begin to understand how many of us want the same thing, and use it as a marker to deem ourselves worthy, or different.

Of course, both Ivy League applications could have used recommendations. Mr Tata is known to help and support students academically if he knows them enough and believes in the applicant. I only requested the one for Harvard Business School. It was too embarrassing to reach out to him and I contacted his office instead, emphasizing as strongly as I could:

'Please ask Mr Tata to recommend only if he believes I am qualified enough to be recommended. I leave it to his judgement.'

The office got back quickly and Deepthi tried to put me at ease by letting me know that Mr Tata would be glad to help.

It was an honest recommendation. Not decorative, not exaggerated, not understated, and true and limited to how much he knew me. It was not a push nor an insistence. It was simply a statement of what he thought of me. A letter that I revisited every other day, but not too much, out of fear of ruining how special it was, or how much meaning it carried.

I have known Shantanu both personally and professionally, and in my view he is someone who has an analytical mind, and his perspectives are insightful. These strengths will undoubtedly be honed in an MBA program with a competitive environment.

I believe he will make a meaningful contribution to the business world following his graduation.

I don't know what my expectations were, but they were exceeded by a lot. He had taken the time to sum me up in just two to three very clear sentences. Clearly, he was observing me, studying me. That was the first of the many times I was introduced to his eloquent writing—brief but pregnant with meaning, and a testimony to his highly observational nature.

Never ever make the mistake of thinking Mr Tata misses a detail. Never. He will remember when you had a bad hair day at work, wore your watch on the wrong hand, or made what spelling mistake on what memo on which day. He remembers conversations and letters from years ago verbatim, and with dates. He will bring up a mistake you made ages ago if you're acting too smart. There are no exceptions to this.

I did get an interview call from Harvard. But to my delight I got one from Cornell too, *without* a recommendation. Through brochures and pictures, all I knew about Cornell was that it was situated in a small college town called Ithaca, cosily tucked away in the hills of North America, and that all its buildings looked like castles.

The interview prep was nerve-racking. The closer you get to something, the more painful rejection is going to be. We got a suit stitched at Raymond's, a first for me. While Naina picked out the material, I found out how expensive it was going to be. It was almost ten thousand rupees. He would be spending a small fortune! But what if no schools accepted me? I would have wasted his money and the suit hanging in my wardrobe would be a harsh reminder of it.

The interviews were held at the Taj Lands End, Mumbai. We had never stayed at the Taj but Naina booked us a sea-view room there for the night. Our small window overlooked the coast and I wished I could be in a state of mind fit to enjoy it. I felt bad because I knew he must have stretched himself thin to book us this room. With every grand gesture that he made, I felt even more worried about letting him down. It seemed like he was living more in the moment than I was. I couldn't spare thoughts for anything other than the interviews.

He tried his best to encourage me to be in the moment, pointing at exciting cafes and listing all the features the Taj had, one of which was the butter soap that we later got addicted to on an unhealthy level. (We took the two soap bars home.) It was an enveloping, creamy, heavenly scent that lingered long after you had used it. With my 'Cigarettes After Sex' playlist playing through the evening and feet propped up in the bathtub, I was in an oasis for an hour, but otherwise it was all about daydreaming my Harvard acceptance half the time and dreading the rejection the rest. Harvard. The Mecca of every ambitious Indian student, no matter which course.

The next morning, with Naina taking pictures of me all the way down to the interview room, as per Amma's mandate, I went in. The waiting room was full of people older than me. The illusion of having the best suit in the world melted away pretty quickly. Some candidates looked like they had kids. Or were CEOs. And they were! A strange train of thought started. If I screwed this up and got rejected, would Mr Tata still respect me? Would he think I'm worth less than what he made me out to be? What does he associate himself with Harvard rejects? I suppose the Indian education culture had led me to believe that my self-worth first lay in academic achievements and then everything else.

It went as well as it could have. But my work experience was not as substantial as that of other candidates. I had just started out. That was probably a red flag for Harvard. The school average was five to six years. I fumbled trying to talk about that, but the interviewer just scribbled in the notepad. I tried to fix it but she kept scribbling. Damn scribbly notepad! I showed her the Motopaws collar I was carrying but she wasn't interested beyond a two-second glance. Walking out, it was hard to tell how it went. I emailed Mr Tata that it went very well, which was clearly, clearly a semi-truth.

The thirty-day wait to the results was the longest, slowest countdown I've ever had to endure. With the apparently not-so-bad interview, the Motopaws story and the recommendation from Mr Tata, my parents had never considered a possibility other than acceptance. I had to get in. The night of the results I was shivering, and at about 2 a.m. we huddled around the overused family laptop.

While we value your application, we regret to inform you that ...

More than the silence, I could feel my parent's disbelief pressing down on me as we all stared at the screen, as if it would suddenly say, 'Just kidding, you got in,' and all would be well. That did not happen. The rejection stayed. The suit, the hotel room, the fees for my tuition, all came back to haunt me.

I was now a Harvard reject.

4

Leaving on a Jet Plane

My reactions were very television drama-esque. With transition effects, slow motion, heart-wrenching music, the whole works. I wrote to Mr Tata like my world had ended and I was betrayed by the universe and there was nothing left for me. Childish, I know. Writing to one of the most respected men in the country with personal goings-on nobody really cares about. It's funny how I live up to all the respectful, gentlemanly etiquette while communicating with him even today, but at the same time when something life-altering happens, he has a front-row seat to the private screening of 'Shantanu: A Millennial Drama'.

I wrote my heart out. And he called to try and tell me it wasn't me, it was them. But where have we heard that before?

'Hello Shantaa-nu? I am really sorry to hear about the rejection. But do not be depressed. It is not the end of the world. You can always apply next year. Harvard never makes any exceptions, that is just how they are. Maybe next year you can apply to many other places.'

I apologized for how ridiculous I was being, bothering him with this.

'No, no. You are like a younger brother. If you are upset, we can always meet and talk about it.'

I did not take that offer. Yes, I wasn't taking this rejection like an adult. But I wasn't going to throw this fit sitting across from him.

He tried his best to show me how trivial this setback would be in the grand scheme of things, that this was a hiccup in getting to something greater. The softness of his words had the warmth of wisdom. He was right, of course, but I had to find that out for myself eventually. At that moment I was married to the idea of going to the best business school in the world. The best. That is what my entire educational culture growing up had unhealthily pointed me towards. The best, or nothing. To be honest, looking back, I don't know if that was the right way. The laughing classroom played in the background like the canned laugh track on the sitcom that was my life, only meaner. I didn't move on. I wanted my toxic relationship with Harvard. I even gave a back-up interview at other business schools, but I lost interest when I got through. If I was going to get my MBA once in my life, if I was going to handcuff myself to a student loan I would pay forever, I wanted to be exposed to people from around the globe, hear their stories, their lessons, their perspectives. An institution our family had never come close to before, because there was no way we could do it twice. It was a single moonshot.

If I wasn't already at my worst, Sukrut got accepted to the New York Film Academy. I mean, I love him but how dare he? There is no greater pain than watching your best friend

getting ready to leave without you. On one of those mopey nights we were at an outdoor bar, him euphoric about getting in, not giving a single thought to making me feel better. I had given up on Cornell by that time. I didn't know why another Ivy League would have anything different to say. Checking my mobile phone for Amma's inspirational messages was now a nicotine-patch habit. As sad as she was about me not having gotten what I wanted, she never let it show. I checked my phone again, but this time at the top of the notifications was an email titled 'Admission Decision'.

Dear Mr Naidu, we tried calling you several times, but could not reach you. We are happy to inform you that ...

I had got into Cornell.

'Sukrut!' I punched his arm hard—out of joy but also to let out my anger at his being a cold-hearted ass the whole time we were there. After seven minutes of Amma happy-sobbing through the phone, I called Mr Tata to ask him if I should accept.

'I think you should. I believe Cornell has a great business school.'

Providential dispensation is such that nobody is ever truly happy. But at that moment, again, I truly was. Funny how Mr Tata has been around for all these moments. The following week, I was madly downloading pictures of the cosy, tucked-away castle-world of Cornell and sending them to everyone for instant appreciation and gratification, as is the world of virtual validation. I was successful in both because it truly is a dreamy place. Naina wouldn't stop talking about how it was an Ivy League to anyone willing to listen. That was the promise I made him, and it felt good to have delivered. As grateful as I was and always will be for Mr Tata's Harvard recommendation, I was secretly happy I could get into Cornell without one.

After what were days and days of just euphoric joy, reality slowly and inevitably made its way into our celebrations. The cost of leaving creeped up on me, and not too slowly. I was losing time with someone whose warmth I had only just begun to enjoy having in my life. We wrote to each other whenever we could—about leaving for Cornell, about how Motopaws progressed, about my dog Brownie, about new innovations, and about Tito and Tango. Eager to see Mr Tata before the days ran out, I planned a day trip for my young Motopaws members to see him in Mumbai. After having scaled across the country, the team had sort of earned it.

I love dress codes, and every other Motopaws drive has had one. This trip was no exception. The dress code was white. There were newly printed ID cards for everyone to wear. Everything possible was done to be presentable at the house of Mr Tata. We booked a tour bus to go from Pune to Colaba, onboard which I was a bit of an ass really, an annoying unit leader throwing instructions at the team that I, at the time, believed were critical. In retrospect, I'm not so sure.

Remove your footwear to the right when you enter.

Don't ask for personal favours.

Don't take pictures.

Don't giggle.

Don't talk amongst yourselves.

When we were halfway there, he called to tell us he was sick that day. Disappointed but worried, we offered to cancel.

'No, no. There will not be another time when all of you are in Bombay. I'd love to see you for a few minutes.'

This might seem like a small gesture, but I would like to emphasize now, and a lot many times in these pages going forward, how much keeping his word means to Mr Tata. No matter what the inconvenience caused, no matter the time restraints, no matter the expense, when a promise was made it had to be honoured.

The bus got quieter the closer we got to Colaba. I herded the young team off the bus and into the house in a sort of single file. Everyone actually did behave. Mr Tata was so amused by the fact that we had brought a whole bus to him. We didn't even have anywhere to park it. He didn't talk much, being his usual shy self. No face was familiar to him other than Sukrut's and mine. But he did make his adorably awkward, witty comments that day. He was in the 'I'm clueless what to say but let me try anyway' zone. After a lot of squeezing to get a grinning Mr Tata and every bus passenger in the same frame, we captured a memory and left. With all of the eighteen hearts full, our bus returned to Pune.

In the few months between that trip and my departure, I saw my parents grow quieter. Amma was all over the place,

trying her best to mask it. Leaving the nest is probably normal for many of you, but I had never stayed away from home for the twenty-four years of my life. I had never changed cities, let alone left the country. There was no stamp on my passport. My parents' whole life revolved around me. From the stories of their colleagues' sons and daughters, they knew that kids who go to the US seldom return. Torn between the reality of that and the pride they felt about someone from the family going abroad for an education for the very first time, I could see them struggle.

I thought about this a lot. I also thought about how it was Motopaws that had brought me all this way. From the first plump, collared dog to crossing paths with Mr Tata, to having a team in every city, to telling this story in my application essays. How I had enjoyed trying to solve something that had been unsolvable for the longest time.

I thought about how much fulfilment it gave me trying to hack something everyone else had given up on. How I was at my best when doing just that. Only in India is there a breed of problems which, if solved, could affect communities of millions at a time. The opportunities of a developing economy and a large population: there's so much that can be done.

My notice period at work was coming to a close. The office had been kind to me. I cannot think of any other workplace accommodating someone's efforts to leave the office so much. On my last day as design engineer, after coming home from the small Tata Elxsi office, I hung up my white shirt with the blue Tata emblem on the breast pocket. That fated, overly worn shirt. It wasn't mandatory at work at all, and I had often been called out as a smart alec for wearing it.

But for as far back as I can go into my childhood, every evening we had waited in the window for Naina to return from the Tata Motors factory and he always wore black or navy trousers, and always the white shirt with the blue Tata emblem, which slowly became clearer as he approached the house. I had only followed suit. Was all of this just going to be an emotional story in my application essays? Was I that superficial? Or inauthentic even? Was this the end of Tata being a part of our family heritage?

I could have left home for good. I just didn't want to any more. I never wanted to, but now I was sure. I wanted to return. No matter how many times I had been told that moving out was a part of 'adulting', I wasn't convinced. If someone had spent twenty-four years making sure I got to this point, invested all of their heart into shaping me, chiselling me to make me the individual I was, it felt selfish to abandon them under the guise of 'better opportunity', especially when their pain was so obvious. I do not have a problem with people who do that, who create a life elsewhere. They have different ways of making it work. Their emotional strength, their family strength must be of a different nature. But it wasn't for me. I belonged with the problems here, with my people here. It was my turn to give them the comfort of company and care. And when it came to Mr Tata, I didn't want to sit half the world away and be his pen pal. He was much too special for that. You don't come upon a friend like him only to leave him behind.

I didn't know how I could bring these things together, though. Plus have a salary decent enough to cover my student loan payments after graduation. I hadn't gotten any scholarships at Cornell. It is hard to get those when you are a last-round applicant. My entire education was based on debt. In the year and a half that I had a job, it was very hard to save anything worth its name, especially for a ginormous expense such as this.

After some very motivated homework, I figured it out. I wanted to be a part of the Tata Trusts, the philanthropic crest jewel of the country. The Trusts have their sleeves rolled up and hands dirty in every social issue one can think of. And as was my recent realization in Motopaws, dirty hands gave me joy. Mr Tata was and still is the chairman of the Trusts, although retired from the chairmanship of the Tata Group. I would be in Mumbai, close to him, to family, doing something that I could add value to.

I didn't know if it would help me repay my student loan, but that was okay. I didn't know how or when, but I would cross that bridge when I got there. Maybe I'd stumble across it, or dangle from it for a while, but I'd cross it. I knew I would.

It was my turn to make him a promise. All of this of course rested on the assumption that I would qualify to work for him. I needed him to know these thoughts. But this couldn't be written in an email, nor conveyed over a phone call.

David Bowie's 'Heroes' played as I lay in bed staring at the worn-out Tata shirt that hung in the dim glow of fairy lights. I thought about how I would be absent from this room. About how my dog Brownie would cope after I suddenly disappeared for the first time in his short lifetime. About how Amma would spend the evenings without pulling my

leg or asking me about my day, trying not to call me and tell me she missed me constantly. About how Naina would have to take care of her emotions and his even more.

There was now time left for only one more Mumbai meeting. But that's all I needed to make him one final promise.

You don't go away from the lighthouse, you go towards it.

5

'Step Out of the Car, Please'

IN MY FINAL EMAIL to him in India, I requested a few minutes to say goodbye in Mumbai. It is not easy to see Mr Tata. A confirmed appointment is a privilege, especially at the last hour. His calendar gets blocked months in advance thanks to the wide spectrum of commitments that include everything from business to friendships, to helping young start-ups, to accepting guest-of-honour invites from different governments, municipalities, philanthropic initiatives and board meetings. All of this on top of his responsibilities as chairman of the Trusts.

To my delight, he replied with an invitation to a farewell dinner. I had underestimated how quickly our relationship had grown over a short time.

I let him know I would be at the Strand Hotel in Apollo Bunder, and that I would see him at his place for dinner. I arrived dressed as best as I could in the Brooks Brothers shirt that I had bought after noticing he wears those too.

(This involved a lot of squint-eyed staring at the logo on his shirt during our previous meetings.) Of course, a half of my final month's salary went in buying just one shirt. I guess when you have to look good, money is secondary? (It is not. I felt very broke and my parents were not okay with this purchase.)

Despite the large expense I did not look good. I was terribly sick with a cold and a fever. I reached his place a little woozy and kept my sentences short because long ones made me cough. Amma had planted cloves in my pocket to chew on so I wouldn't have a coughing fit when talking to him, but they ran out even before the evening began.

'Let's go out for dinner to my favourite restaurant, the Thai Pavilion. I'll drive.'

That is the only time I have seen Mr Tata drive. He used to back then. He doesn't as much any more. Some of his cars are convertibles. But since he loves to drive with the top down, he gets mobbed often for selfies and pictures. He loves driving, that much is true. And I am only hopeful of sitting beside him on another occasion again. With the cheer and charm of a welcoming host, but not with a lot of conversation, he drove us to dinner.

When we reached the Taj President, the crowd parted to make way, but only at the last minute because he never makes his presence felt. You would never know when he is in a building or a lobby. You would just stumble upon him walking past you or in your direction. He never made any special requests, rarely called ahead for special arrangements, never had a bodyguard and never asked for security. He didn't bypass ordinary protocol for guests the way the staff usually suggests he should. Despite everyone's best efforts, he insists on being treated exactly as any other person at any given time.

'No, no. I'll go through security,' he told them as he put his wallet and keys in the tray, and I followed. His favoured table, where he doesn't get mobbed a lot, was set aside. We sat across from each other and my whole focus was on not coughing. The last clove I had I swallowed whole by mistake and I was out of ammo.

It was a quiet dinner for the most part, the exact opposite of what I had imagined it would be. Silences are the longest when you have the most things to say. That's the thing about building anticipation—too much is too bad. I wasn't accustomed to being in the company of, well, a celebrity. I was sick. I was sad. I was going to leave him. And I was awkward. We made small talk for as long as we could. With whatever little appetite I had, I tried my best to empty my plate.

Towards the end, when he was ordering dessert, I found a part of my voice and a few shreds of courage.

'Mr Tata, I had something to say.'

'Go on.'

'I have given this a lot of thought ... and ... I want to come back. I want to work for the Trusts after graduation. I want to help solve issues that the Trusts are trying to solve. I feel it is where I could belong and contribute the most.'

Silence.

I hurriedly added in a single breath, 'But please consider it only if you think I'm worth having at your organization, if you think I'm capable and can offer value to the Trusts.' He put down his spoon slowly, the true embodiment of suspense.

'I am so happy to hear this, it would be great to have you work for the Trusts. But there will be many opportunities abroad that you will come across and would want to explore. Don't decide just yet.'

'I know, Mr Tata, but my mind is quite made.'

'Well, why don't you go to Cornell and, closer to graduation, if you still want to come back to the Trusts after exploring all your interests, I would be happy to have you. I just don't want you to feel trapped because of the promise you're making right now. In case you find a better opportunity, I would want you to have it.'

'Okay, Mr Tata. But I'm telling you, I already know.'

'I am delighted to hear that. By the time you graduate it would be a great time to join the Trusts, and the organization will be much bigger.'

'But ... Mr Tata ... I would not want to take this forward if you think I'm not capable yet.'

With his large hand on my shoulder, he replied, 'You are not. There is a sincerity in you that's somehow ... different. And business school will polish you, teach you what you need and give you so many perspectives. When you return, we will put you on a track to solve the right things.'

I took a bite of the ice cream with the appetite that had just been reawakened by this validation that I did not buy one bit. That fault lies with me.

'Will you come for my graduation?' I joked to break the tension, a shameless and hopeless request.

'If I can, I definitely will. Probably a day before the ceremony. It's too crowded on graduation day. And either too hot or too rainy.'

The weight of the words said over the last few minutes hung over us. It was hard to know back then how saturated with significance they were and how they would later come to shape my life.

'I might see you in New York in December,' he said. 'We can go out and explore the city. Maybe we could go watch a movie? I'm never able to go to movie theatres. People keep mobbing me, even in the loo. The last time I went, my sisters had to come rescue me. We could go if a good one is playing.'

If only you knew the effort it took to maintain my composure at the thought of all this.

'Sounds perfect, Mr Tata. I would love that!'

It was only three years later that we did, in fact, watch a movie in a theatre. It was at Sterling Cineplex, at a screening in Mumbai, not in New York.

If I look back at everything he said that night, I think he had figured out how scared I was to leave. I can see now how all the things he said were to make my departure less scary for me and to leave me with a hopeful bunch of possibilities which would make this seem less of a farewell. It was his way of saying goodbye without actually saying it. I wasn't sure if we would be able to do all the things he said. Most probably not. But that was okay. Only listening to him gave me strength. After all, at one point in his life, he too had left his home behind for life's next steps. He knew how it felt.

There was no way I could stop the two years of distance from unfolding. I had to come to terms with them. But that didn't mean I couldn't share my life in New York with him.

'Would you mind if I kept you posted about my life there?'

'I would love that. You could message me whenever you feel like it.'

I am positive there have been at least a couple hundred times when he must have regretted ever saying this, because, boy, did I abuse that privilege.

On our way out of the Taj, a few strangers stopped us. Some to say hi, some for pictures. I took the pictures while he obliged. Little did I know the number of times I was going to have to take his picture with countless strangers over the coming years.

He offered to drive me back to the Strand Hotel. I insisted on taking a cab, but it was pointless.

'No, no. It's door-to-door service.'

On our drive back, people recognized him through the car window. Some would wave, some would ask to shake his hand. But he never pretended to not see them. He has this peculiar way where he gently raises his hand halfway and waves back, always.

We pulled into the hotel driveway. I managed an awkward goodbye and stepped out. He didn't. Right before he started up the car again, all the pent-up goodbye emotions did their thing. I went around the car to knock on his window. He lowered it, curiously staring up at me with those wrinkled, wide Ian McKellen eyes.

'Could you step out of the car, please?'

To this day, he jokes about how he has been the most responsible driver possible throughout his entire life and has never been pulled over, but he believes, in that moment, I gave him that experience anyway.

I hugged him as soon as he was out.

I was so happily sad. I felt I wasn't entitled to this mix of feelings.

'I will always be here, friend.'

I watched him drive away through my watery contacts against the backdrop of the parked, blinking Apollo Bunder yachts bobbing up and down on the harbour. I was sick. I was sad. And I was happy. It's hard to explain. You can spend the longest time preparing for a goodbye and it'd still hurt as if you didn't see it coming.

How lucky to have someone it was so tough to say goodbye to.

Bittersweet is a beautiful feeling to write about. Not so much to feel.

6

Ithaca Is Gorges

THERE WAS NOBODY at the bus stop. The only thing heavier than the ginormous two suitcases was the lump in my throat. It should have been long gone after the overwhelming farewells at the airport. Amma was very brave, fighting back tears till the very, very end. Her entire world revolved around me. Sukrut, my great-grandmother, who was the proudest, Naina and a few close friends were there to see me off.

And then, Tuhina, this girl in Mumbai I had absolutely fallen for right before leaving. I'd like to think I did a fairly good job of keeping it together. It was only when the plane took off and I read the goodbye letters she gave me that the lump in my throat gave way. Something about looking at cities from far above makes you feel insignificant yet gives you heart. It amplifies everything you're feeling. The two classmates travelling with me got to witness, awkwardly out of the corners of their eyes, or rather right in front of their eyes, a very sloppy breakdown as I soaked the letters in my hand. It was a heartbreak music video without the music. A wonderful start to the journey that was Cornell.

I didn't know where to go from the bus stop. My Indian mobile number wasn't working. The taxi took me roughly to where my room was, and helped me call my new roommate. The sickness from when I met Mr Tata had gotten only worse. Cough. Cold. Fever. More cough. So much cough. I knew one is supposed to be taking in this completely new world with all its awe and first-time experiences, but not dying took away from it quite a bit. Vivaan, my new roommate, found me, and while I didn't know much about him, I was ready with my 'I'm new to independence' narrative, with an obvious plan to co-depend the hell out of him emotionally.

The minute I got an American connection I called Tuhina. Most of the initial days I lay on the bed talking to her, hoping to recover with the help of an assortment of cough drops, variations of Tylenols and home-sent antibiotics classified according to symptoms by Naina. Vivaan would go out on hikes and meets to introduce himself to our new classmates as they arrived in Ithaca. It felt like I was already missing out and school hadn't even started. More and more time was spent with Tuhina on the phone as I recovered as slowly as possible. She was my only connection, holding the cup at the other end of the string.

From the first day of school to the last, for every single day of the two years at Cornell, I could never not be awestruck by how magical the university campus was. Eighteenth-century stone buildings with towers and bells, blossoming bushes and trees. Hills covered in shades of green I had never seen before. All possible Hogwarts fantasies came alive there. Cornell had a school for everything! Engineering, music, architecture, business, law, name a discipline and it had its own pretty heritage building with character and a story behind it. That was the dream written by Ezra Cornell, and what the university was known for: 'Any person, any study'. The business school was no outlier to this architectural feast. It was brick red, and again, a castle. It was called Sage Hall: the only building I never came to love very much, except from the outside.

You could stand in the middle of it all and try to take it in, in a single go, but you just couldn't. I was anxious Cornell would fade away from my overwhelmed, volatile memories and written descriptions would never do justice to its charm. The desperation to document all of this in the two years that I was going to be there was peaking. So I decided to log my life there through two mediums, quite at odds with each other: Instagram and Polaroid pictures. I went on adventures

around the campus capturing everything. My classmates, however, barely left Sage Hall. I tried dragging Vivaan once or twice on my exploratory Shire journeys but only succeeded once. He gave up after finding a girlfriend. (I had a little something to do with it but no regrets.) Throughout my time there I posted about Cornell so avidly that the school invited me to be one of its social media ambassadors. The administration knew me by my social media handle before my actual name and I'm not sure if its bragworthy or just awkward: @suitcase_full_of_sparks, after my favourite song by Gregory Alan Isakov, and I wasn't really sure if that was a good thing.

I guess at this point in the story, a confession is due. The fact that I'm writing this book only validates what I am about to say. I like to capture experiences. But what I love is to share them. It's not a popularity thing. It's a character trait that is so fundamental that when I experience something beautiful, I want everyone to experience it with me.

When I learn a lesson, I want to tell the story. If I find a song I can't let go, I can't wait for others to listen to it. My life is an open book (now quite literally). This makes a lot of people uncomfortable, who insist there should be some part of you and some experiences that you keep only to yourself. But those parts come as they do, and I can never consciously keep things to myself. It is extraordinary that people who don't know you get to be a part of your story. They can be at Cornell with me; they can meet Mr Tata with me. They can stare at the flower I stared at and laugh at what made me laugh. The joy of that unified experience pushes me to share. It's just so ... wholesome, to know there are people you will never know who have lived your life with you without even being there.

As I almost recovered, school started soon after and orientations were overwhelming. Each person in my class was a genius in his own field and a hero in his own story back home. What none of us anticipated was how it would feel when we finally arrived at an Ivy school and found out that everyone was an apparent genius. You weren't special any more. Everyone had been hand-picked and had gone through rigorous rounds of examination. Complexes were raging. I was in the youngest spectrum of the class, and I look way younger than my age, which is not a good combination given the fact that most Americans look much older for their age. I often got the 'Kid, are you lost?' look and it was hard to be taken seriously. I had to answer the age question a lot. And while it was annoying, deep down I believed it was what set me apart.

We were taught how to roll our 'R's and emphasize our vowels to make sure we would be understood when talking to recruiters from big firms. It's something that I vaguely picked up but let go just as quickly. I didn't want to sound like anything other than what I actually sound like. We were taken on beautiful wine tours, had inspiring speeches from the dean and were put through a nauseating number of group exercises. Business school is all about getting to know everyone and getting the art of networking embedded in your DNA. And while I respect that, my social anxiety was peaking. We learnt how to tie tie-knots and wear our suits, how to write professional emails, how to have a firm handshake, the appropriate cuff length outside the coat sleeves and a list of mannerisms that would determine whether the great corporate houses of America would want us at all. Words like 'gravitas' and 'synergy' flew around a lot and I'm not so sure anyone knew what they actually meant.

But everyone's origin stories were extremely exciting. They were exactly why I had made this journey. No two stories were the same. There were shoemakers, musicians, bootstrapped entrepreneurs, chefs, army veterans and the list goes on. While uncovering their stories, I was laughing, smiling, talking to everyone who crossed my path, and I was getting truly inspired. But the one thing I wasn't doing was making any friends. Surprising, because it had always come very naturally to me. I didn't understand why it was different here. It was tough to figure out whether it was the culture, where you can only scratch the surface of a person in the first few meets, or if I was isolating myself unknowingly. Everyone was getting along with everyone, as if they had known each other for ever. Groups were forming already but I was outside of them all. Even my roommate started going out by himself without inviting me—something that was a product of his independence but that my dependent self couldn't comprehend. I felt betrayed.

It was lonely and disappointing to have ended up like this. I had daydreamt of making lifelong friends in the first week at Cornell itself, friends who would attend my wedding some day, and here I was without one solid person I could call anything more than a classmate I could talk to. My only outlet was Tuhina back home.

We were constantly on the phone. Even when I went to social gatherings, I didn't really mingle and ended up on the

phone next to the bouncers outside the door. The one or two people who tried to make me comfortable started giving up on me as I increasingly disappeared to make these calls. I used to describe Ithaca to her. Sent her pictures of everything new to me and wrote to her while she slept, only to cover up how badly I wanted to give it all up and come back. I had only just arrived but was already counting down the days till I saw her again.

These phone calls quickly turned to fights. Tuhina would just disappear for days sometimes. With the opposite time zones, the distance and her absences, I found myself locked in. It felt like I was no longer as much a need for her as she was for me. The phone calls got shorter, and the fights longer.

In all honesty, I expected her to rescue me from everything that was going wrong at Cornell. In the largest learning curve of life, I was using Tuhina as a crutch.

In the end, no matter how well you think you've designed a dream, or how great an architect you think you are, you don't really end up with the version you want. And it is silly but amazing how we continue to be surprised when this happens. I was supposed to be a brilliant young mind with tons of friends and adventures there. Instead I was a sappy, sick let-down, stuck in his own bubble over someone miles away, letting down Amma, Naina and everyone who had supported me in getting there, especially Mr Tata.

Ithaca was a dream, far more beautiful than how
I had dreamt it to be.

But I just wanted to wake up.

7

'Can I Stick My Tongue Out?'

WHEN YOU'RE PUT in a place that's so far out of your comfort zone, either your underlying courage and strength shine through or you use one of the many unhealthy defence mechanisms that your personality has to offer. For me, that mechanism was recreating my Indian life in New York. And after getting tired of running after buses I was seldom able to catch, the first recreation, a rather unconventional one in the US, was to get a motorcycle.

I went on many test rides with random owners off Craigslist and classifieds with no luck. Some were too expensive, some too heavy. Some way out of town. It's not as easy to buy a motorcycle in the US as it is in India, even more so in the sleepy town of Ithaca. There are no showrooms strewn across the city, and not many mass-manufacturing motorcycle brands. In New York, everyone had pre-owned legacy motorcycles or bulky Harleys I was repulsed by. When I was almost ready to bury this idea, a botany student at

Cornell who was moving to Vancouver invited me to see his motorcycle.

It was a 1978 Suzuki 550GS and by far the most historic and well-kept piece of machinery I have ever had the privilege of owning. Strapping cash together was tough, but all it meant was surviving on ramen for a few months.

My batchmates could not get over this.

'It is dangerous, and you will die!'

'Why would you not want to be safe?'

'Do your parents know?'

It was annoying to go around explaining how severely misunderstood everyone was about the motorcycle culture. It pretty much equals death for most Americans and these taboos were outdated. Cornell's archives showed that the last and the only motorcycle club in its history was in 1924. There was no information on what happened to the club later; it mysteriously disappeared. There was no paper trail nor did the libraries have any records.

I thought Cornell deserved to have a motorcycle association. The sum total of people who sort of got behind this idea was one. He was a senior at Cornell, owned a red Ducati and happily agreed to be on the board. If I haven't emphasized enough how big a deal motorcycles are in the US, the local newspapers proved my point when I founded the association.

INDEPENDENT SINCE 1880

The Cornell Daily Sun

FEATURED IN CATEGORY

October 28, 2016

New Club Aims to Revive Motorcycle Culture

By Ronni Mok

The Cornell Motorcycle Association is once again starting up its engines. After an undefined relapse, the original group – established in April of 1924 – is reopening to both Cornell students and members of the Ithaca community.

Beyond the organization's founding date, the club's history is a mystery, according to Shantanu Naidu MBA '18, the organization's founder and president.

"All we have in the archives is that there was a Cornell Motorcycle Club 92 years ago and I tried to find the termination date in the archives and I talked to all of the researchers," Naidu said. "Somehow the termination reason and date is unclear, we just know that it got discontinued and nobody knows why or when."

There were, of course, other smaller forms of this coping mechanism. I went ahead and got a guitar, just like I had back home in India, and started amateurly performing at open mics. I had a safe set of about three songs that I played one Tuesday every month.

I filled the apartment with fairy lights and clichéd posters, always had ambient music playing in my room, and set up a small library on the wall, like Naina had helped me set up back home.

I wasn't strong enough to go through the learning curve that pretty much everyone goes through. But, to be honest, it felt safer gathering these bits and pieces of my life, bits and pieces of me. I don't know if it did what it was supposed to, but each decision led to a story that I can tell today. If I had not gone through all of this, there would be no motorcycle association, no midnight conversations in our apartment with people who came for the fairy lights and music, and I would never have performed on stage. Little did I realize that with each desperate decision to cope, I was creating pockets of experiences I could narrate when it was all over, like I am now.

For the first time in a very long time, survival felt like a possibility.

If there is anything to be said about the promise of keeping Mr Tata posted on my life at Cornell, it would be that I might have really abused that privilege.

But the point of sending him updates was not that I had to get a reply. It was more for me than for him, to find comfort in knowing that a friend back home knew how my days went. I am close to my family, sometimes a bit too close for comfort, but there are still things I couldn't share with them. He still maintains that it was a delight to open the overloaded chat window, full of hyper-descriptive texts and vivid pictures about life in Ithaca. But the thing about an empath like him is that you may cause him whatever discomfort and he will never let it show.

Sometimes there were one-line responses, congratulations if there was an achievement, motivation if I was down, or just quips about pictures of my suspiciously clean apartment likely being staged. Many rainy Sundays he would call when it would get lonely to the point where he would ask on the phone, 'Is it a rainy, lonely Ithacan Sunday again? I have had a lot of those myself.'

Texting is such a millennial practice. But it gave me the space to express myself honestly without worrying about how I sounded or came across, something that's difficult on a phone call or in a meeting.

In this sea of exchanges, there was one I had been waiting on.

Dear Shantanu,

Congratulations. You have really made a mark at Cornell in a very short period of time. I look forward to meeting you in New York City. I expect to be there some time in October or November '16.

I must say that I am very proud of what you have been able to do and the way you have made yourself a part of the campus.

Warm regards,

Ratan

I was excited at the thought of being in New York City with Mr Tata. Would I finally get to see Central Park, most of which I had only seen in Hallmark Christmas films? Would we catch a movie? Would he get bored? Would I goof up? I counted down the fall days.

Everyone has their own layered relationship with New York City. It is a relationship with a living being, an actual person. Each visitor has their own version, their own narrative.

Everyone is hustling, trying to make it, whether in life or through the day. It is overwhelming to be on the sidewalk with people who are always anxious to be somewhere. When everyone around you has a purpose in the city, it is lonely to be there without one. Fortunately for me, my strongest connection with New York would always be the days spent with Mr Tata near Columbus Circle, overlooking Central Park.

I got on the bus from Ithaca to arrive in the city a night before he did. There was not enough in my pocket to afford a hotel near the Pierre, where Mr Tata would be staying, or anywhere in central Manhattan. One of my friends from Motopaws, Revika, who led the team in Navi Mumbai, let me stay in her matchbox apartment. As soon as she found out it was my first time in NYC, like a proper New Yorker, she quickly took charge of giving me a taste of her nuanced experiences with the city. She took me to restaurants tucked away in Chelsea, on boats parked by the river, sneaked me into rooftop bars in Manhattan, pubs in the meat-packing district. Nobody else could have introduced me to the frequency of New York the way she did, because that was her version of the city, and I felt privileged that she would share that with me. I left for the Pierre the next morning.

The Pierre: a heritage hotel owned by Taj Hotels on Columbus Circle, with the elegance of a luxury hotel but the welcoming warmth of a New York apartment. A typical Manhattan facade, but somehow different. Eager bellboys waiting by the door, hailing taxis and greeting guests with generous smiles. I loitered around the lobby awkwardly, but one of them recognized who I might be.

'Mr Naidu? Mr Tata hasn't arrived yet, but you can wait for him here. Right this way.'

I followed him down the royally carpeted lobby, passing large hallways lit with antique chandeliers and mural art.

Half an hour later my phone rang.

'Hello Shantaa-nu, I'm sorry I kept you waiting. Would you like to come upstairs? I have just arrived.'

'Of course, Mr Tata. I will be right up.'

The moment I saw him open the door, a wave of pure, homely warmth swept over. It was not that long ago that I had seen him drive off into the Mumbai night, but it felt much, much longer. I didn't know if he still appreciated hugs, but my levels of awkwardness had spiked to new highs. I just shook his hand instead.

His window overlooked all of Central Park. It hadn't snowed yet, but it was a grey New York sky, the kind pluviophiles romanticize about.

'This is the first time I'm seeing you in a jacket. You look positively smart.'

There was so much to catch up on. Cornell. Mumbai. Dogs!

I. Spared. Nothing. Except, my lonely days at Cornell. He was the first person from back home I was meeting and I should have told him everything. But somehow between being completely honest to the friend I had found in him and fearful of being judged as not strong enough, I didn't tell him.

Halfway through my monologue, I could sense something was off. A part of him wasn't there in the room. He was masked in a cloud of concern and worry. After debating whether it would be appropriate to ask, I blurted, 'Is something bothering you, Mr Tata?'

Something was. It turned out that the issues around the then leadership of the Tata Group, lawsuits that he is still fighting in 2020 even as I type this, had begun in some form. He reminisced about the time he took over as chairman—JRD (Jehangir Ratanji Dadabhoy Tata) had been a non-intrusive mentor and guide, and, with Mr Tata's and the group's best interest at heart, had pointed him the right way and suggested course corrections when needed without mandating that they be followed. Mr Tata had valued JRD's ambient presence in the office even after his retirement. In fact, Mr Tata had used JRD's vast library of experiences whenever in doubt. Mr Tata too wanted to be a guide whenever he was called upon or needed, but his intentions were misunderstood and it did not work out that way.

One of the other things that occupied his mind often was the future of the businesses that had been acquired or nurtured during his time. It's hard to forget the sentence that came after, because it gave a glimpse into his underlying drive to find solutions:

'We don't sell broken businesses, we fix them.'

This was the first time I was introduced to the conflict that was soon going to take over his life in the worst way possible, a conflict I would see play out in the years ahead quite closely.

What a terrible person I had been. Over all those months I had bombarded him with the goings-on of my life, but I knew so little of the challenges of his, until now. Almost out of guilt for having opened up about his problems, he suddenly jolted:

'Come, let's get dinner. Do you like Italian?'

Like Thai Pavilion was his go-to place in Mumbai, he had one in New York too. It was called Cippriani's. It was only a block away. We decided to walk it and, as usual, he didn't fuss about calling ahead for a table.

'Hope we get a table; it's always full.'

And it was. A jam-packed, small, classic New York joint, with an '80s Hollywood vibe hanging heavy on the loud conversations in a room full of old money and legacy fame. It was classy enough to intimidate you. Suits were tailored and dresses were red-carpet ready. It was almost anti-climactic, since the place was so small the waiters didn't have room to walk sometimes. He might have been the simplest-dressed person there. A blue shirt and a windcheater.

While I struggled to get through the panic-ordered chicken, he didn't say much. Clearly, our conversation had broken the dam of thoughts surrounding the struggle he was facing.

I let him be. It is bothersome when you are deep in worrying thought to have to force a normal conversation out of courtesy. I did not want him to feel that compulsion.

We walked back in silence. A few minutes later, I suggested I leave.

'Oh, before I go, I wanted to show you something.'

I took out the not-so-compact Polaroid camera out of my shoulder bag and saw his eyes widen.

'It's a Polaroid camera.'

'I thought they don't make those any more. That looks like it's from the past. We have digital cameras now, Shantaa-nu.'

I explained to him how Fujifilm had revived the Polaroid hardware in a millennial context.

'Can you take a selfie with it?'

'Well, technically, you can, you just wouldn't know what you're capturing.'

'We could try,' he said, amused.

I turned the camera around and he closed in on the frame and a big flash went off. He was not expecting that.

'That was ... so bright! I can't ... I can't see anything.'

We watched the Polaroid develop. 'I look like a floating head.'

We were both out of focus, with puffy front-camera faces, but we had just captured our first New York memory. A first of many Polaroids.

The next morning, it felt like I was with an entirely different person. He elegantly went through his English muffins, while I wolfed down the hotel's signature strawberry cream waffles with very little shame and was stared at by him during the entirety of this meal. They were a refreshing change after the barely edible cooking I did back in Ithaca and cups of ramen. During his visits in the future, it became a bit of a ritual. Every time we had breakfast at the Pierre, he insisted I have the waffles over anything else. It was all worth it to see him grin ear to ear.

We spent the day doing things that, according to his flight crew, were routine for each one of his New York visits but were new to me. The first stop would be at a Macy's, to choose bed linens and buy duffel bags. He did not miss being recognized everywhere he went. Special attention has always made him uncomfortable, which can be tied both to his shy, introverted self as well as a desire to be treated like a regular person. Having said that, even in New York, wherever he went he had a person at the shop who always assisted him as a regular. He would get special attention not because they knew he was Ratan Tata, but because every time he had

walked into that store he had been the kind, gentle regular that he always is.

The next stop would usually be a pet shop. Tito and Tango loved these very specific transparent baseball-shaped balls with smaller tennis balls inside. But they tore through them so frequently that he restocked during every visit. That, with some very specific treats, and we would be out of the pet store.

The third stop would probably be a Barnes & Noble. Discussing bestsellers, some business magazines and a lot of looking around. One of the greatest books I have ever read was recommended by him at that time. He tried his best to buy it for me in New York, but they had run out of copies. Eventually I bought us both a copy, and it is one of the most emotionally charged books I have ever had the joy of immersing myself in. It reflects strongly what moves him, hinting at the vulnerable innocence at his very core, which is a far greater part of him than the industrialist everyone knows. *The Art of Racing in the Rain.*

The next stop would sometimes be at a Brooks. He would pick out one or two shirts, mostly without a pocket. I had only one Brooks shirt—the one from Bombay—he had the exact same one, and we had both coincidentally worn them on the same day several times, only to look like very inefficient valets. When he found out I had ripped mine on a nail, he hunted down the same one in the store. It was a futile fight at the billing counter over who would pay, no matter how hard I protested. He shut down the argument with classic finishers like, 'Can't I give my friend a shirt?'

The legal battle that was soon to take over his life had not hit with full force yet. He was a real goofy, witty, random character to hang out with. One time at a store, I was taking a picture of myself in the mirror, being the vain self that I am, when he popped up beside me.

'Would you like to be in the picture, Mr Tata?'

'Can I stick my tongue out?'

'I don't see why not.'

And so he did stick his tongue out.

The final stop would be at a popular technology store on Fifth Avenue. While most of the visits were mainly to buy mundane things like a phone cover or charging cable, I noticed how he always keeps himself updated with the latest hardware, where anyone else his age would likely have given up on learning new things by now. He refuses to not keep up. It was delightful to see him set up face-unlock on his phone as he moved his head from side to side and up and down.

The hours flew by in these stops across the city and before long it was time for him to return to India.

It was always sad when he left New York. Every time he got into the car, this big fat lump would slowly rise up in my throat and I could never hide it—like the time when I turned around at the airport and saw Amma wave goodbye.

When his car turned around the kerb, I watched it leave and texted him how sad it made me to see him go. I dragged my large suitcase, walking towards the dingy Port Authority, towards reality, with the burden of being an outcast waiting for me at Cornell, wading through a city whose hum felt alien the moment he left. My phone pinged with a message from Mr Tata.

'I'll see you soon, my friend.'

I couldn't help but realize how blessed I was, to have been in one of the most beautiful places in the world, sharing the company of an affectionate friend who made time from his many commitments for me.

Today I can say this with conviction. The city was what it was. But for me, the city was always him.

He was the largest part of my New York City story.

8

Bom-bae

MONTHS SEEM LIKE years when you're on your longest and toughest learning curve. Six months were all that had passed since I left home. Returning to India for the winter break, however, felt like returning with an unexplained wife and two kids.

It was meant to be an exciting end to the year. Christmas, family, Brownie and a lot of mental housekeeping. But, most importantly, even in the midst of the chaos and controversy that had erupted over the exit of the Tata Group leadership, Mr Tata made sure I got his very large-hearted invite to be a guest at his Colaba house for three days to catch up on everything before I returned to Ithaca. I was looking forward to time with my friend.

As much as I was dying to see everyone, I caught myself thinking about Tuhina often. She was, after all, my introduction to Mumbai. In kaali-peelis, walks by the sea and secret nights of intimacy rested all my memories of Mumbai. I feared spiralling into the nostalgia of our time in the city. But she was out of town. That, and Mr Tata's invite, kept me from falling into the rabbit hole.

Those days hold some of the warmest memories I have of my time in Mumbai. The wholesome spirit of the city had put a charming filter over everything. Christmas lights in quaint Bandra streets, decorated churches, pleasant winter scents, docked boats on Apollo Bunder and golden-hour evenings. Decembers in Mumbai can bring a sense of belonging into the heart of someone who has never even been to the city before. I spent half a day retracing my steps in the lanes behind the Taj. The colonial buildings separated by timeless, dilapidated mansions, ageing gracefully, second only to good wine, or Meryl Streep. It is not uncommon to suddenly find yourself romanticizing Mumbai, never even remembering when you began.

Close to sundown, it was time to go see him. It felt like the privilege a student experiences when his professor treats him with the same care and concern outside of the classroom as inside, or when Mitch Albom would go see Morrie. The kaali-peeli got there early, but I didn't want to go in and seem too eager. Six p.m. was the given time, and I wouldn't go in any earlier or any later. All these self-made rules, this discipline, were a product and result of his being in my life. He made me want to be perfect, made me want to be honest. When you're in the company of someone as black and white as him, your greys get washed away. In the same white shirt from our first meeting, I went in at 6 p.m.

The house is a very accurate depiction of Mr Tata's personality. Named 'Halekai', Hawaiian for 'house by the sea'. A dominantly white colour scheme, minimal articles on display, with a whole side of the house made of windows alone, facing the coast. No grandeur in the colours, paintings or in anything in the rooms. 'Pure' would be a good way to summarize the theme. His long-standing caretaker informed me that Mr Tata would be late and showed me to my guest room. He was in the office in Fort dealing with the legal battle. But still, rather selfishly, I wished for him to return so we could catch up on so much.

My fiddling with the remote on the bed accidentally made the automated blinds move up slowly, revealing a balcony, opening to a beautiful old spread of trees in his back garden.

The last few golden-hour rays came straight through. The French song 'Equation' was playing. The smell of winter leaves was thick in the humid sea air. I lost myself in a sweet euphoric daze, staring at the little white Nano parked below. I was thankful for where I was. This had stopped being about the privilege of knowing Ratan Tata a long time ago. It was now about a person I had come to value, respect and learn so much from.

The sun set and the lights came on. I let the blinds down, peeking through, still waiting, until a black car pulled in. It was him. I only had a few seconds to straighten my shirt and attempt to comb my misbehaving hair.

'I'm so sorry I'm late, Shantaa-nu. Was that you in the balcony?'

'Yes, Mr Tata ... that was me,' I said.

'Come, let's go see Tito and Tango.'

This wasn't the first time I was seeing him, nor the second. In fact, it wasn't even in the first five. But every time I met him, it took me time to adjust to his presence. It is very tough to not say or do something stupid when you meet him after a long while and are in awe that this is, in fact, Ratan Tata.

We sat on the lawn facing the sea, playing fetch with his two gentle giants. As distracted as he was because of what was happening at work, he took plenty of effort to be in the moment, especially with his dogs, even though I wasn't expecting any. We would get interrupted by calls every few minutes about legal developments that were coming like darts from every direction possible. It was starting to become evident that Mr Tata was going to get little or no relief till this long-drawn fight was done. The backlash was going to last for years, and get uglier before it came even close to dying down.

I was just happy to be there. I wished I could help him get through this mess, but I couldn't imagine how. It is an unpleasant feeling, sitting there helpless while the suffering of your friend is on display in front of you. After dinner at home, he gave me a tour of the house and we ended up in the library, the picture of Tito and him taken by Sukrut still on the mantle. He went around pulling out books and showing me pages.

'Didn't you say that your business case competition was on rural housing?' he asked.

'Yeah, for the slums of Mumbai.'

'Let me show you something.'

He pulled out a book on architects of the world and flipped through the pages looking for something intently. It was Moshe Safdie, an Israeli Canadian architect known for Habitat 67, the model community housing complex in Montreal, Canada. Mr Tata explained how Mr Safdie was famous for his modular design houses, reinventing spatial utilization in his architecture.

'I'm not suggesting this can be used for our slums, but some version of this definitely can.'

A very important thing I have observed with Mr Tata is that when introduced to an innovation, the uniqueness of the innovation in itself isn't always a thing of awe to him, but a societal problem that could be solved through the application of this innovation is. In this case, Moshe Safdie had designed the modular settings for apartments in general, but Mr Tata found it interesting only in the context of applying it to Indian slums.

'Why don't you come with me to the World Trade Center office tomorrow. You can see the slums surrounding the campus from the twenty-sixth floor. It is a disturbing difference, a mismatch of classes. But you can also see how organically they are mapped, how there is pattern to the chaos.'

He explained how change is difficult in slums because the dwellers don't have legal papers for their huts. Entire slums are run by slum lords who are impossible to trump.

'You could have the most innovative housing design—in fact, we already have those, made out of molasses and renewable materials and such—but what is the use if we cannot get past the slum lords?'

I felt inadequate for not being able to answer. I wasn't expected to, but sometimes reminders would kick in that Ratan Tata was asking you a question. I didn't know then how accommodating and encouraging he was about diverse opinions and discussions. I was only focused on using carefully measured words and replies that did not give my insecurities away, or make me sound arrogant, or anything in between. (I no longer worry about this today.)

We lazed around for a bit, flipping through news channels. He had had enough of the legal issue broadcasted all over the media and skipped through it. I could see him try very hard to be there for me as a host and a friend. He really was trying, but his distraction was inevitable, and justified. I could tell he was tired, and I did not wish to burden him more with the worries of entertaining me.

'I'll see you in the morning then, Mr Tata?'

'Okay, would you come up for breakfast?'

'Sure. I'd like that very much.'

'I'm sorry I don't have the strawberry waffles, but we can have something else.'

'Anything would be fine, Mr Tata.'

'I'll take you to the Trusts offices tomorrow. We will try and figure out where you could fit in and contribute to the Trusts most when you graduate, based on your Cornell experiences so far. We could also try to shortlist a few non-profits in the US where you should apply for an internship. It would be good for you to get that exposure before you return.'

In the middle of his own storms, he still cared about this? I imagined myself in his shoes, and questioned if I would have done the same. Anyone can offer help in the best of their times. Very few can when their own troubles weigh down so heavily. He doesn't have to try. Empathy and sensitivity come naturally to him.

There was no way to fall asleep after the day I had had. Just then my phone buzzed with a message.

'I'm coming back to Mumbai tomorrow. I really want to see you.'

It was Tuhina. I stared at the screen. I was staying with Mr Tata. He was the reason I was in Mumbai. After all the hurt and pain that had been the long-distance relationship, I couldn't put that above him.

'I really want to see you too,' I typed.

9

Smooth Criminal

AT 8 A.M. THE NEXT morning, we were on the deck on the third floor overlooking the swimming pool. With the textbook definition of bedhead, he complained about how he had tried everything to keep the pigeons off the pool but with no luck. This was followed by a very animated narration of all his attempted solutions, listed one after the other.

I was very excited for the day. He had decided to take me with him wherever he went. The list of the wide, and random, variety of subjects not connected to each other that we debated is still fresh in my mind. His witty perspectives made everything so much more amusing, as if you were given new perception glasses. It was like having your own personal Mr Miyagi, but instead of asking him one life-changing question, I had plenty. The speckled sunlight, old trees and the Victorian buildings were a blur outside the car window as the happy day breezed by.

Our first stop was his office in Fort where I got to see Deepthi again. The same Elphinstone building where we first met. The three of us huddled together to write introductions to some non-profits in the US where I could intern and get relevant experience before coming back. He was really investing himself in curating these different situations where I would learn a lot. However, of my own choice, I ended up interning at the Tata Trusts in the summer, for the animal hospital project that had been his and the Trusts' long-standing dream. I didn't feel it then but can see today that it was a bit of priming of sorts. It was embarrassing and awkward to sit there listening to him dictate my 'strengths' in front of me. Just how you feel when everyone is singing the birthday song for you and all you can do is either stare at an empty space or right back at them till you shrink of embarrassment into a wrinkled raisin. On our way out we passed a tiny cabin. An insignificant, tiny, cosy cabin filled with scattered files. There was no way of knowing the role of that cabin then, and what it would mean in the time to come.

The bullpen office of the Tata Trusts is located at the World Trade Center in Cuffe Parade and is always alive with activity. Two awkward employees sat down to interview me for the different areas of work that the Trusts were involved in and went through my resume to figure out where I could contribute the most and be of value. There were so many burning issues to solve and all of them were exciting. Housing, health, nutrition, and all of them had a direct Trusts presence. Though, when asked about my skills, my answers were corny, business-school replies that we were taught so well at university but didn't really help anyone. I could sense the tension at the Trusts given the legal mess that was ongoing. 'I hope there will be a Trust when you return' was a chilling statement someone made when I was there.

Before we headed back home, Mr Tata called me into his cabin to show me the slums around the World Trade Center from the twenty-sixth floor window, as promised. He pointed out the trickles through the slums, which were clearly the walking routes, the density, the pattern, the retrofit. The order in the chaos, the stark difference in classes highlighted by where we were standing and the contrasting standard of life a few hundred feet away. He is genuinely adorable when he talks about something so devotedly and with conviction, and rural housing is definitely one of those causes close to his heart.

On our way home he mentioned there was a visitor coming over to see him and that he would have to excuse himself. Not checking my phone when he was around was a personal rule

I followed strictly. As soon as I was back in my room, I went through my messages.

'I'll reach Mumbai by midnight. I want to see you.'

'I want to see you too. But you know where I'm staying.'

'Just for a few hours?'

'I'll try.'

I wanted to see her. After months of distance, fights and all the ugliness, I missed her. For me, Mumbai was her. I wanted a blurry night again. I wanted to remember what it felt like to be completely drowning in her company, to be close to a friend. To see the wind in her hair when the kaali-peeli drove on the sea link.

After mustering enough courage and clearing my throat a suspicious number of times at the dinner table, I managed to emit sound.

'Mr Tata, I had a small request.'

He looked up.

'Umm ... a friend of mine is leaving for his master's in the US. I was wondering if I could go see him off?'

'At night?'

'Yes, the flight is at 1 a.m., I think. I'll go at midnight.'

'Flight to the US?'

'Yes.'

'Which flight? I didn't know there were any flights at 1 a.m. to the US.'

'Umm ... I'm not sure.' And it was in that moment I regretfully realized the depth of his knowledge about pretty much all the flights leaving Mumbai.

He chewed on his food and the silence was painful. This

was going very wrong. I couldn't tell if he was buying it or bluffing or neither.

'Okay, of course you can go.'

Had he seen through that terrible lie? Did he think I was taking him for granted? I couldn't read him at all. After dinner we sat talking for a while, about everything that had happened through the day, but he was clearly tired.

'Okay, I better get to bed. Are you going to come back really late?'

'Yes, Mr Tata. If that's a problem I can stay back.'

'No, no. Here, take my key card so you won't wake anyone up when you're back.'

He was being extremely sweet, which was breaking my heart even more. It was all cool-dad, big-brotherly vibes as he handed me the key. After showing me where to tap on the wall to open the door, he went to bed.

I was supposed to feel bad in that moment, and to some extent, I did. A unique, blessed destiny had brought me to that house, to him, and I was putting it all at risk. But I had to see Tuhina. If there was any guilt to come, it hadn't arrived yet. Not in its entirety anyway.

I left as quietly as I could. She was waiting outside. From across the street under the yellow streetlight, she waved. Nothing had changed. Her scent took over the moment we hugged, and our worlds collided. From leaving tearfully on the plane with her letters in my hand, to hanging on to a rather thin thread all the way in Ithaca, I had missed her all through. I didn't know how badly I needed this until just then. But I had to stop midway, trying to usher her into the cab quickly so

the security guards won't have a story to tell the next day. The night went by as we traced our steps on the same roads, lanes and alleys as before I left the country, holding on to each other in the same way, in that same yellow taxi. I loved Mumbai, but Mumbai with her was always an overwhelming cocktail. Suddenly we realized we only had thirty minutes left. Nostalgia consumed our remaining time far too quickly.

From the time I had hugged her till the time I had to leave, it felt like one fluid moment.

I had forgotten why I was in Mumbai. There was still no sign of the guilt that I knew was due. Strange. Lost in the high of the past few hours, I reached Mr Tata's residence at 3.30 a.m. It was too dark and I tapped the key card he had given me in multiple places, but no door opened. To an outsider I would look like a confused, horribly incompetent burglar looking for a door that didn't exist. After a solid few minutes my hand accidentally passed the right spot and the door opened. It was only after hitting the bed and setting the alarm did I remember what she had said to me.

'I want to spend New Year's with you.'

'But I'll be with Mr Tata.'

'I don't know when I'll be seeing you again. Please?'

'I ... I don't know.'

'Please?'

'I'll try,' I said once again.

Breakfast next morning was one of the largest moral conflicts in my short time as an adult. The lie, as predicted by several metaphors in the English language, was snowballing.

'Mr Tata, I'm afraid I will have to leave by midday today. My family would want me to be there on New Year's Eve.'

I know. How low of me.

It might seem ironic that given how close I considered us to be, I couldn't tell him the truth. Deep down I knew just telling him where I was going would be okay. But I was afraid of offending him by choosing to spend the day with someone else instead of him. And yet, I was doing exactly that.

'Oh ... I wish you could have stayed longer, but I understand.'

His goodness twisted the knife in my heart.

I packed my bags. Took a final look across the room. Out of the window. Smelled the Mumbai winter again. I told myself I deserved a day with her before leaving the country again. Someone I had stayed away from painfully, someone who had tried her best to be there for me from across the world, someone I would most likely lose again the moment I returned to university. It helped me set the guilt aside, even if just for a little bit.

He came out to see me off at the door.

'Goodbye, Mr Tata. I hope I will see you in New York again soon.'

'Goodbye, my friend.'

Do you hate me right now? Because I sure hated myself. I wanted to drop everything and tell him the truth. Tuhina was important. She was right up there with everyone else who helped me survive Cornell. With Sukrut, Mr Tata, my parents. But wanting to give her a final day, not knowing if I'll see her again, wasn't a mistake—the mistake, I realized, was lying to him. He would have understood, I knew he would have. After having shared so much of my life with him, I did not have to lie.

It has now been over four years since the day I left him at that doorstep. And I still believe that, in that moment, I

was, and will always remain, a little bit heartless. I can't help but be angry at whoever I was back then, to have taken for granted the best thing that could happen to me.

As the next few hours and the next few years showed, the half day that I got was wonderful but I couldn't forget what I had sacrificed. Tuhina and I separated the moment I was back in Ithaca. All those December adventures were unable to save our relationship. They were a way to rekindle the spark from the past. But that was probably exactly why I knew I needed to go see her, a final goodbye.

But what has endured and grown over the years is Mr Tata's affection, his paternal camaraderie and his companionship, always unconditionally present. At the time I started writing this chapter, I could no longer carry the burden of having lied to him. It was time to confess.

'Mr Tata, that December when I came to stay with you in 2016?'

'Oh, yes. That was a lovely time.'

'Yes, it was. But ... I lied to you. Please don't be mad.'

'Tell me.'

I narrated everything, sparing no detail.

'Oh, you scared me. That's entirely forgivable, my friend. I thought it was something far more sinister. Please don't even worry about it.'

He never brought it up again, except when he taunts me sometimes when I'm leaving work in a hurry: 'Oh, are you going to see your "friend" off at the airport?'

I can't rewrite what I did in the December of 2016. I wish I could. But I guess things had to happen that way for me to come to a lot of realizations.

What I can do, and have done, is never lie to him again. Fortunately, I never have to. Anything that I can tell myself, I can tell Mr Tata, and, more often than not, I do. The next year when he visited New York once more, I went to see him from Ithaca again. Only this time, instead of keeping things to myself, I told him how lonely I was abroad, how I hadn't found belonging where everyone else had.

I had finally found the courage to say, 'Mr Tata, I'm not okay.'

And he sat there and listened, promising me it was going to be okay, and he was there till it was.

If I could go back to the December of 2016, I would still be the twenty-four-year-old, emotional mess who just wanted to see that girl one last time. But I would look him in the eye and tell him the truth, and I know he would understand. Because honestly, I cannot remember a single time in all my years with him when he hasn't.

10

Thinking of Winter

IF YOU TRULY WANT to marvel at the plays of destiny, the best place to find them would be relationships. Look at the people closest to you, the most special ones that changed your lives, and see what beautiful sequence of coincidences had to take place for them to be in your life. But this little story, the happiest one of my life, begins with a rather simple fact: I was lonely.

I didn't know enough about depression to be able to say if that was the case. I still don't but try to educate myself. I concluded that my sadness was tied to the fact that with a semester in, I had no friends to call my own, nor any comfort in those I met and saw every day, and I was seven seas away from where I belonged. What was so different in Ithaca from home that I found myself in such a rut? In the endless comparison of my two lives, one difference was obvious: my dog, Brownie.

Brownie, because every part of his body, eyes included, was chocolate brown. Brownie was a stray picked up from the streets. A strong, independent dog and a devotee of affection and sweetmeats. A dependable figure in our house just by his presence. Resting your head on his belly as it heaved up and down was the equivalent of a spiritual cleanse. He was getting older as I was studying in the States. If nothing else, if nobody else, I thought Brownie would have helped me now. But he wasn't there, and he wasn't going to be. And then I thought the two words that can only lead to great euphoria or terrible disaster: 'What if ...'

I don't know who the architect of the universe is, but he did create something that we, as a race, can rely on, eyes closed and hearts open: dogs. Ithaca was a small town. And as I scoured the web for a sign from the universe, all I could see was breeders selling dogs. Breeders went against everything I stood for and everything that got me here. They are often referred to as puppy-mills where female dogs are tied down and forced to breed until they can no longer give birth and are then put down or abandoned. We have rescued such poor throwaway mother-dogs at Motopaws often. Shelters, on the other hand, had a lot of eligibility prerequisites that I wouldn't meet. For example, you couldn't be a student. Other factors were profession, landlord information, nationality, etc. A student is not looked upon as someone responsible enough to adopt a pet with special needs. I understand why, of course. I wouldn't get a chance to explain how my half-day school schedule and proximity to the university was a good parenting environment. As I thought about how bad an idea this was, at the bottom of the computer screen I saw a different post.

'Family puppies in Moravia. Please drop by for a visit or call xyz.' It was accompanied by a picture of a couple, their daughters, and the family dog with her litter. Moravia was Ithaca's neighbouring town. It wasn't exactly nearby. It was thirty miles out, an hour away. There were no buses going there. And I had never ridden that far. Drifting off into a trail of possibilities, I fell asleep.

The entire next morning at university, I was only physically present in class.

'Should I?'

'Nah.'

'But then ...'

'But I can't ...'

'But I could have ...'

'Maybe if I ...'

'That's impossible ...'

It was torture. I wished I had never thought of this. I wished something made it impossible for me to consider doing this. I even tried talking to a few critical people, who weren't very hard to find.

'Man, you've already made one impulsively blind decision getting that motorcycle. Please don't do this.'

I get it. I'm a student. A puppy is a responsibility. I might move. I have drafted adoption forms preventing people like me from entering the adoption pool. Yet, the more each person told me not to do it, it only made me realize I could do it.

It was fall. The evenings were beautiful but chilly, and the sunsets were done by the time you got home. The last class that day was microeconomics. Professor Waldman taught that class. A rather important class. Everything he taught was critical. I was not in that class.

I was on my motorcycle, going sixty miles an hour on a dirt road towards Moravia, with the sun about to set. There were no clouds of thought any more. There was nothing. There was only the beautiful fall road, and the chill that announced winter was near.

My gloves from India weren't riding gloves and my hands were frozen. I couldn't feel my fingers and I wasn't too far from a frost bite. I parked but couldn't pull the key out of the ignition. Squatting next to the exhaust, I tried warming up for a few minutes. There wasn't a soul around; it was dark but the lights inside the house were on. It was time to go knock, but I didn't have to. Someone had seen me.

'Shantanu?'

'Hi, yes.'

'Oh, my god. Did you ride out in this weather?'

'Yes ... Yes, I did.'

'Wow, let's get you warmed up.'

By the fireplace, with a warm cup in my hand and the crackle of a new fire, I was just happy to be alive, to be honest. The family was quite homely. I do not remember their professions, but I remember that they didn't intend to turn this into a business, and that this would be the first and the last time their dog would be having puppies.

Soon enough, logic started beating the living daylight out of deciding to ride out here on an impulse.

'What *was* I thinking riding out here?'

That train of thought ended delightfully. To my right a small partition gate had opened, and seven golden balls of everything pure came tumbling out.

'I'm afraid, you're a bit late. Six of the seven have been taken. There's only the one left. He's not getting adopted for a while now. I'll be honest and tell you he's not like the others as much. But still a sweetheart. I'd be happy if you got him off our hands so we can go back to our normal lives.'

'Which one is he?'

'The one sitting between your feet.'

A face stared up at me, then down again, then up again. Well, more fur than face. His giant puppy head was so heavy that he couldn't keep looking at me. I took him in my arms and put him in my lap, belly up. There was nothing wrong with him. Not that it would have mattered anyway. So much hope in his eyes. So much wonder. So much confusion and curiosity, yet so joyful. Every responsible cell in me questioned what I was doing. And then he let out the tiniest of barks. And I smiled. Not the usual smile. Not the 'how cute' smile. A genuine

smile. An unexplained smile. And I didn't remember the last time I had smiled that way. Unknowingly, but with meaning.

'Mr and Mrs Banks? I'll take him.'

The next few moments were a blur. He wasn't two months old yet, so legally I wasn't allowed to take him. There were two weeks left. With a permanent marker they wrote on his collar: 'S.N.'

Permanent.

'You have a home now, bud. I'll be back,' I whispered in his miniature ear before riding back. The chill in my gloves was no longer a match to the warmth in my heart. It was a slow, cold ride on dark roads back to Ithaca. But it didn't matter. I had a little light of mine. Ithaca was known, famously or infamously, for its winters. I had already decided that this dog would go wherever I went in the whole wide world, without exception. But to never forget where he came from, I wanted a thread that tied him to this place. He would be called 'Winter'.

No, I obviously did not go get Winter on my motorcycle. I don't have to tell you what kind of wait those two weeks were. The beds were bought, the bowls, the cute collars, the food, the training books and puppy pads were all ticked off the checklist.

Among the one or two people I could count on was Wen Ko, an isolated introvert from Taiwan. We used to sit together in places with less conversation and long silences. Comfortable long silences. In my journey with Winter, Wen Ko was always there for me, for him. She drove us to bring Winter home.

The fall noon was gorgeous. The house was even happier than the last time. Winter was the only one left there. All the other ones had been taken. After wishing the family well and with a ball of floof in my lap, off we went! His head was out of the car pretty much the whole time, and he snapped at the air off and on, trying to eat it. Silly, goofy polar bear. Wen Ko had a hard time keeping her eyes on the road.

It took time to fall into a routine with all the classes and walks. I rescheduled everything to be with him as much as I could and still managed my courses well. We used to play for hours in the morning—to the point that he used to sleep while I was at university, without a worry in the world. My senior used to hang with him while I was away. Only my return would wake him up. I moved from working in libraries to working at home. As we started going on longer walks, he would be in my arms for half their duration. The tiny polar bear couldn't walk that long.

It took time, but I started noticing the ways in which my life was changing. Barring a few busy people on the street, everyone stopped to meet Winter. Every. One. I was forced to interact with so many people. Answer their questions: his name, his age, my name. As our route became repetitive, people would hang around certain streets for him to come by. One thing was absolutely clear about Winter: he loved people.

This was a zero-exception rule. If you so much as looked in his direction, he would take that as an open invitation to come up to you. He was sly, though, always preferring girls to guys. The whole 'girl magnet' theory is very, very real. On Friday nights we would get mobbed by drunk undergraduate sophomores running to us, screaming from across the street.

On our way past any Starbucks, the baristas would run out to give him a Puppuccino, which is basically a teeny-tiny cup of whipped cream. With a cream-covered snout and having made tons of new friends, we would return home.

At home, after I was done with assignments, with him staring at me the entire time, we would watch *The Office*. It was our favourite show. He was always dangling off my lap as we both looked at the screen. Other dangle places were knee, chest, legs. Honest to god, it felt like he was watching too. But then ten minutes into the episode, he would no longer be in the conscious world. He was out like a light. One such night, when it was cold outside, and Joshua Radin's 'Winter' played in the background, I stared at him bundled in my lap in some possessed position. Only then did I find the moment to realize how, in a matter of weeks, Winter had already saved me.

I was forced to talk to strangers. Make new connections. Smile at people. Meet some of them over and over. Step out of the house with a purpose. Have someone to look forward to after classes and in life. Where I would have been sitting alone behind closed doors not knowing how to escape the hole, he had brought back the grace and warmth that had been absent for more than a while. It's not like he solved any of what was wrong in my life. But he made me not care. He gave me the courage to face it.

There were other days when I would look at him and feel that all that he had in this world was me. How could I have taken the responsibility for the happiness and health of an actual life? In moments of weakness, I spoke to Wen about thoughts of returning Winter. What if there was a better family out there? What if I snatched a better future from him? But it was time to grow up. Even if it cost me

everything else in life, I would stand by him and never let him feel the slightest bit less loved or have less than what anyone else in the world could give him. Nothing in his future would be uncertain. I was going to make sure of it. I repeated it till I believed it. And it became the truth and reality of our lives.

The big mistake that I had made was to assume our apartment was pet-friendly. Well, it wasn't. Till the time that Winter was little, I used to sneak him in in my jacket. It was a long winter coat, completely protecting him from the cold outside. And he never once let out a noise or barked or yelped. He didn't even squirm. Not once. I didn't understand this. I didn't teach him this. It was almost as if he knew. How could he have not given himself away?

I know for a fact that while it wasn't unsafe, there was no way it was comfortable in that coat for an overly curious fidgety puppy. But the fact that this wasn't affecting Winter and that he wasn't protesting destroyed my conscience every time. Eventually, circumstance decided for us what had to be done.

It is dishearteningly crazy how fast they grow. One fine day when it was getting harder and harder to hide Winter in the jacket, his leg popped out and was dangling. The maintenance man reported us, and that was that. I got a notice to either give up the dog or vacate the premises. And so began our house hunt.

Every day we used to walk up and down the hilly roads of Ithaca, knocking on doors and calling numbers on billboards. Everyone welcomed my tenancy, only until they heard I had a dog. After half a month, one landlord asked if Winter was

a puppy and I said yes. He agreed. It was a typical country house with a sloping roof, and we had the top floor, with a small fire escape and a roof we could crawl on to through the window. At the back was a dense forest and it would get quite dark. I could not have lived there without Winter, who made himself at home from day one. He loved the balcony, and eventually, for better or worse, learnt to watch me come and go for classes through the window. We went on beautiful hikes and forest trails every morning, especially in the snow. Chasing deer and discovering big sticks and branches. Oh, how crazy Winter is about snow, true to his name.

As he grew up, uncomfortably quickly, into the giant that he is today, the number of people stopping to meet him only increased. He still got Puppuccinos, still got hounded by drunk undergrad girl squads, still used his sly techniques to get pets from the ladies. Eventually, he became a class favourite too. In his honour, I took over the Cornell Pets Society to host pet socials on the beautiful grass settings of the university, and soon enough everyone knew Winter.

Yes, that includes Mr Tata too. He used to get frequent photo updates of how fast Winter was growing, and I cherished his responses. Oddly, yet pleasantly, Mr Tata never once asked me how or why I had got Winter. I guess, he just understood. Regardless of whether he was lonely then, he knew about loneliness too, at Cornell and otherwise. He never asked, and I never told. Winter was just accepted by him, as he was everywhere in the world. 'Such a happy, cheerful dog,' is his constant description of Winter, even today, as he rubs his ears affectionately.

The day Mr Tata met him was when he dropped by at our tiny Ithaca apartment on one of his New York visits. Winter was desperate for his attention. But in the spur of the moment, when I opened the window, Winter jumped out on to the roof that he loved so much. Mr Tata was terrified. I crawled out and called to him, but he started moving further back. I had to lure him with fake promises of a walk and food before I could finally get to him. All this in front of Mr Ratan-freaking-Tata. Such a lovely introduction.

When it was finally time to leave the country, I started preparing all of Winter's paperwork six months in advance, with research on the laws of both countries, the airline, the certifications, the problems that could come up, and Winter's well-being through the flight. It was hard to find a proper flight, let alone a gigantic cage for his size. I studied each and every document, requirement, small laws and by-laws for months to secure all loopholes. Stories of horrific travel incidents involving pets put a sword through my heart and I started thinking of finding him a family in Ithaca out of fear of hurting him on his way to Mumbai. But I had to brave it. I knew he wanted to be with me wherever I went in the world, and so did I.

When it was time to book his ticket, I did not even want to risk doing it online. On a suitable weekend I travelled to JFK just to book his ticket, to ask them all the questions and leave no gaps or any possibility of surprises. With the number of questions I had, something I learnt from Naina, the Lufthansa team had to huddle around, explaining step by step what exactly was going to happen on the day of the departure. Only then did I book Winter's ticket.

When the time came, we were on the same plane—he in the cargo hold and I in the cabin. Snout poking out of the grill of his cage, and a 'please don't go' look in his eyes, Winter was wheeled away before the flight, and there was nothing I could do to change it. It was one of those times when you really wish you could speak to your dog, to make them understand. For more than ten hours I sat with gut-wrenching guilt, and worry, knowing he was directly beneath me, but not with me.

Why couldn't I make him understand that it was going to be okay?

Every minute of that ten-hour flight, I prayed for him to be safe, for him to know I was going to be there at the other end.

The thing about imprinting yourself on someone so powerfully, undilutedly, is that without them you feel like you can't breathe, let alone be yourself. All Winter had seen—through his jacket, through the window, through his eyes all day, every day for the better part of his life—was me. I know he is my world, but it's not even imaginably close to how much of a world I am to him.

At customs clearance in Mumbai, I waited restlessly, trying my best not to irritate the policemen, but failing miserably. Everyone was standing by for an update: Mr Tata, Amma at home, Naina outside the airport, my friends in Ithaca and Mumbai, and Wen Ko. After what felt like an eternity, they wheeled him out. I wasn't allowed to get him out till we had left the airport. I rushed his trolley out, and Naina opened the cage. He jumped straight into my arms.

I held him in a tight embrace. 'You will never go through that again. Never,' I whispered in his ear. And I kept my word. I could see it in his eyes, he could never go through such separation again.

As I sit typing this, with Winter at my feet, in our Colaba matchbox apartment, after a day of meeting new people on the promenades, I find the journey we have taken together hard to believe. Joshua Radin's 'Winter' still plays in the background.

I might have made this journey back to Mumbai, back to the lighthouse, but it was long, and it was difficult, and I wanted to give up quite a lot of times, and I almost did.

Winter was the boat that got me here.

11

Aamras

Cornell had a special service to print your graduation invitations, with an embossed emblem, your name, the name of the school you are graduating from, a heart-warming illustration of the university atop a hill, and sealed with wax.

Only two people I knew were coming, obviously. My birth-givers. But I printed some more anyway and sent them to people who had helped me get through these messy years. I knew they'd be there in spirit. Quite naturally, one of the invites was mailed to Mr Tata in Mumbai. As I drowned myself in preparing for graduation, booking the gown, buying the cap, getting the house cleansed and exorcised because Indian parents were on their way, I also got a reply from Mr Tata. He had accepted the invite.

This I had not expected. And it was foolish of me to have not expected it. Two years ago, at the end of that awkward farewell dinner in Mumbai, I had jokingly asked him if he would come to my graduation and he had promised he would try. Now he was keeping his word. I was to receive some awards in a ceremony, and then there was the graduation ceremony. He said he would try and make it to one of those.

I requested my professors to leave a chair empty close to the exit so he could leave when he wanted. What an electrifying moment it would be to have him sitting there when I walked across the stage. I imagined it many different ways, each equally emotional, except the one where I tripped and fell (a very real possibility). To my parents, graduation was no longer as important as the guest attendee. Unfortunately, this euphoria was short-lived. Close to the event, Mr Tata wrote to me mentioning that his departing flight was too close to the ceremony, so he wouldn't be able to make it there.

Of course, I was downcast. But instead he suggested a small graduation dinner the previous night. I asked him to join us at home, and he graciously accepted. My parents went on anxiety trips of intensities known to few. It was Amma's game now. The dinner would be her success or her disaster. Never mind the son's graduation.

What food to make?

What do we wear?

Where will he sit?

We don't have a tablecloth.

We don't even have a table!

The house was scrubbed, then rescrubbed and re-exorcised. Tablecloths were bought, tables were borrowed. We attempted to get rid of Winter's shedding season fur. Clothes were picked out and so was the menu. It was a bit of fish curry, rice and roti. Simple. The tension in the house could cut glass. The day arrived, and I left my squabbling parents at home to go pick up Mr Tata from the hotel.

It was a beautiful Ithacan day. The trees were lush green, the sky was a stark blue, and the town was alive with visiting families. I didn't have a car, so I just Ubered it. Within twenty minutes we were back and he was climbing the narrow steps to my home. I had called Amma to say that we were almost there.

'WHAT! ALREADY? Couldn't you take longer for just this once?' Yup, this was going to be a fun dinner.

I wish you could see the pure, child-like joy on Naina's face when he opened the door for Mr Tata, same as from the day they had met for the first time. And Amma's anxious grin as she rushed from the kitchen to see him, which took like two footsteps because the house was *small* small. It was so small that while we gave Mr Tata the prime spot in the big chair by the window, Amma and I sat on the bed and poor Naina on the old gas heater next to Mr Tata for lack of chairs or space.

Winter was kept in another room so as not to overwhelm our guest with his sloppy excitement and demands for attention. But the moment Mr Tata heard him bark, he was not at all pleased with the fact that Winter was inside all because of him. So out he came, tumbling, and spent the entire evening with Mr Tata and Mr Tata alone. The moment we tried to take him away, Mr Tata would scold me instead. I was a lower priority that day. Complete sweethearts, those two together.

While the food was being prepared, and Naina was nervously chatting with him on any and every topic under the sun, I put on my gown and cap and came out to a delighted room.

'I know you can't come to the graduation, Mr Tata, but since you came all this way, this can be our little graduation.'

He got up. 'Congratulations, Shantaa-nu. You have made me very proud these two years. I am very happy for you, and I can't wait for you to return to Bombay.'

We took early graduation pictures, the only graduation pictures that mattered any more, with Amma and Naina in and out of the frame. It was a beautiful Ithacan day. Everyone I cared about, everyone who had pushed me to get to this point, was in the room. I still had to process the fact that Mr Tata did in fact keep his promise and make time to be there. All our hearts were obviously full, it was time for the stomachs.

The dinner was basically Mr Tata being quiet and smiling and nodding as he went through Amma's dishes while she watched him with an eagle eye, trying to process his expressions to decide whether he liked the food. Her jittery sentences sometimes had to be completed by me while Naina tried his best to make him comfortable. Winter, of course, had chosen him as buddy for the day. Time went by far too quickly with this half-sentence chitchat and Amma's constant servings.

We didn't really have any dessert, or that's what I had thought. But apparently there was something Amma was carrying from India: aamras, or mango pulp. He might not have taken multiple servings of anything else, but it was a joy for my Amma, and for all of us, to see him go through two bowls with great ecstasy. That aamras was validation that the evening was not a disaster, after all. After dinner, like an excited uncle, he showed us forwarded animal videos on his phone. 'Wait, here's another one...' We sat chitchatting, laughing, Winter at his feet, with the heater and the love keeping the room warm and toasty. I didn't care about the ceremonies the next day. As far as our family was concerned, my graduation was already done!

He took our leave, with Winter's fur all over his black trousers. At the hotel lobby, we said our goodbyes, which were really beginnings in a way.

'Congratulations again, my friend! I wish you all the success in the world, and I really am proud of you. I will wait for you in Bombay. And I'm sorry for troubling your mother for the lovely meal.'

On the ride back, I realized how far I had come, how far I had come with him. That evening was not so much a celebration of me graduating as of the people who had helped me build myself.

Amma next to me, Naina on the heater, Mr Tata in his special chair and Winter by his feet: every person in that room had committed themselves to me, my well-being, my growth and happiness. They were all there for me. My journey in Ithaca was complete. The Cornell chapter had ended. But there was no more fear. I had all of them.

On the coast of Colaba, as the waves lapped the tetra pods, the rotating beacon was already lit.

12

Office of the Chairman

MUMBAI.

I have romanticized it enough—to the point where if I do it any further, I might lose you as a reader. But we will have to take that chance anyway.

I had interned with the Trusts already over my summer at Cornell for the veterinary hospital project. Mr Tata's dream project of having a state-of-the-art veterinary facility in Mumbai was taking shape through the Trusts. Given whatever background I had in animal welfare, he thought it best for me to be the bridge between the Trusts and Cornell. I worked from Cornell itself, while the team from the Trusts came to Ithaca, and together we went across the state of New York to visit all sorts of animal hospitals that Mr Tata asked us to see and bring back the best practices from. I worked as hard as I could, took on additional responsibility whenever I could, and I don't know if I was in a position to make a difference to the team, but I kept trying. That and the fact that I had one foot in animal welfare because of Motopaws prompted Mr Tata to have me join the animal hospital team permanently after graduation. It made complete sense.

I had my offer letter. The salary was enough to pay my student loan instalments. That and living in Mumbai didn't leave anything to save, but nothing was wanting. My office was on the twenty-sixth floor of the World Trade Center at Cuffe Parade. Mr Tata does not work out of this office, but the entire Trusts was there. It is the bullpen of the Trusts. The hub of activity and hustle and bustle. The machinery behind any of Tatas' philanthropic initiatives.

I was all set to take on this challenge. It is a publicly known fact that a state-of-the-art veterinary hospital was Mr Tata's long-standing dream, very close to his heart, and to be able to help bring it to life was a proud privilege. Not being at the same office did mean I wouldn't see him there, but I was hopeful that he would make the time to catch up every now and then. At least we were in the same city.

For Winter's sake I wished to live close to where I was going to work. All the house-hunting was done in Colaba. The rates there are as high as in New York! And just like New York, all of them were matchbox apartments. Many houses later, in one particular flat, the real estate agent pointed through the window and said, 'And across the street is where Mr Ratan Tata lives.'

Of course. How could I have missed it? The flat was small, barely a one-room kitchen, but had large windows with lots of light, and was directly across the street from Mr Tata. It was too heavy on my pocket, and still is, but the thought of

being closer to my friend was heartening. Maybe we would meet often, maybe we wouldn't. I took it anyway. At least it was right by my office.

Colaba, one of the seven islands of Mumbai, was leased to the East India Company by the British Crown in the 1600s. It became a commercial trading hub and is full of beautifully built British buildings that still stand, some well kept, some withering. The boundaries are lined with seaside promenades such as Marine Drive, Apollo Bunder, Back Bay and nostalgic architecture now occupied by the head offices of almost every major company.

Colaba is considered a posh place to stay and work and people who grow up here are often referred to as 'townies'. Millions of people in Mumbai travel for at least two hours every day to their workplaces. Trains, buses, walks. It is a true hustle. In Mumbai, it is a privilege to be able to live in a place just a few minutes from where you work, that too in a place as beautiful as Colaba, or 'Town' as the rest of Mumbai calls it. All this made the tiny one-room kitchen quite okay.

In the week leading up to the first day of work, I explored Town on foot. I spent my time visiting all the old museums, the seaside promenades, the cosy little cafes, art galleries and restaurants; discovering buildings that looked like monuments but housed everyday businesses; and, of course, people watching. The busy energy coursing through the veins of Mumbai is no myth. It is electric and addictive. I had waited too long, much too long, to be here. Every place I explored and every moment I spent there reassured me of having made the right decision.

I finally belonged again. I had no complaints. As I stood on the Marine Drive promenade, looking out to sea, with the salt on my lips, lines of swaying palm trees on both sides and a clean blue sky above, I realized nothing was wanting in the life of Shantanu Naidu. I was privileged, and I was grateful for it.

My phone rang. It was Mr Tata.

'Hello Shantaa-nu, how are you? Have you moved to Bombay?'

'Yes, Mr Tata. I am all set and will be joining office next week.'

'Okay. I called to tell you something. I know you are placed with the animal hospital team. But ever since Venkat left to be at the Trusts, there has been a place and responsibilities left at my office. It can also be a bit difficult managing things by myself. I would like your help in managing the office and

with the Trusts' work and start-ups. Would you be okay to work with me from my office and assist me there?'

My legs wobbled. I had to sit down. I took a deep ocean breath. 'I would ... I would be honoured, Mr Tata. That would be ... at the Fort office?'

'Yes. You can still support the animal hospital team. I will come in next week and show you the ropes.'

'Okay, Mr Tata. I'll see you then.'

I didn't realize the weight of that phone call, of those brief but pregnant words.

I had just been enlisted in a little piece of history. The plan had been clear so far: graduate to join the Tata Trusts office for the veterinary hospital project, and meet him every now and then. But I couldn't process what had just happened or what it meant. I just sat there replaying it in my head.

I went on my first day in a kaali-peeli, listening to my meticulously handpicked inspirational playlist, trying hard not to move, to not let my shirt get creased even a little bit, which is near impossible with the humidity in Mumbai. The Elphinstone building was still majestic, with the Horniman Circle garden on the right, St Thomas Cathedral in the front, the Bombay Stock Exchange on the horizon, and other British-era Venetian, Gothic buildings around the circle largely occupied by the head offices of renowned banks. The streets were always alive with lawyers from the high court, interns trying to make it and executives pulling up in their long black cars. The air was thick with the familiar scent of opportunity.

I was prepared to enter the Trusts, I had prepared for a long time, but as a soldier doing his part and contributing to the big picture: building a veterinary hospital. What I was not prepared for was to be enrolled in the direct service of a Tata. 'I work for Tata' now had a whole different meaning. I did not know what my duties would be. I did not know what this position warranted. You couldn't exactly look it up online on Glassdoor. Every moment since that phone call was a cocktail of adrenaline, euphoria and anxiety, with the little umbrella of happiness tilted on the rim. All this against the backdrop of the beautiful chaos that was south Mumbai.

Mr Tata's office had three employees, and now I was the fourth. I know I've spoken about them but, trust me, their descriptions will only keep evolving through the pages of this book.

There was Deepthi with the short pixie haircut, the stern little soldier.

There was Parizaad, the veteran assistant manager who has been with Mr Tata from the Bombay House era.

And Denese, the front desk assistant.

They helped me set up office and showed me to my desk, and I was pleasantly surprised when I discovered I sort of had my own tiny cabin. It was the same tiny cabin I had walked by years ago when leaving the office, not realizing I would be occupying it some day. It didn't have a view or window but it was nestled tight in the middle of everything. The peons were asked to empty the drawers and clean up the furniture, and the IT team scurried to get my system set up. With every added person setting things up for me, I felt more and more guilty and embarrassed. I think this was also because it was a ten-person office at best, including the support staff, so everything that was done was noticed and highlighted. All I had expected was a corner cubicle. I stood by quietly in the corner of the cabin

with a limited vocabulary of 'Yes, ma'am' and 'It's alright' or 'That's really not necessary'. But the way Deepthi and Denese helped me set up, making sure I had everything and welcoming me properly without any 'new person' resistance, I took it as a reflection that Mr Tata's values percolated into the people who assisted him.

He had already called me twice to see if I was set up. I think he was also slightly anxious about defining my role for me in a single day. Until the time he arrived, I had confined myself to the cabin, having the guts to ask only half the questions I really needed to ask, like where the washroom was.

In a couple of hours, I heard the office door open but I couldn't see who had come in. I knew it was him from how quiet everyone got and stood up before he reached my cabin. He beckoned me to follow him into his. After a little small talk, he got straight to it:

'I am meeting a start-up in a few minutes, and I think you

should join me. Here is the pitch deck; you can go through it. It's a shipping industry start-up.'

Well, damn. The meeting was in a few minutes. No orientation, no onboarding.

It was a start-up that was aggregating supply chain logistics in commercial shipping. My goal was to sift through the papers and retain relevant information, enough to be able to add value to the meeting and understand what was being pitched. I had barely gone through the deck once when the two founders walked into the waiting area. I went through the deck again. Within seconds, I was called in.

It was a very powerful moment. I was sitting next to him with the founders across us. And as they started their pitch, I couldn't help but notice the weight of the fact that, two years ago, I had sat with Sukrut in those exact two chairs, discussing Motopaws. What a wild turn of events to be now sitting on the other side, next to the very man who had invited me then. Destiny is too poetic for its own good, but I love it.

Mr Tata isn't one to wait till the end of the presentation to ask questions. He asks them as soon as they come to him. And while some start-ups get unsettled by this, the ones that can assimilate what he is saying and answer are truly prepared. At university, our venture capitalist judges would stop you right in the middle of the presentation and ask you a paralysing question. But that's just how it is. Time is precious, and comfort zones are outdated.

As the number of questions he asked kept mounting, the answers were not as satisfactory, which led me to have follow-up questions that I kept to myself.

Was I supposed to interrupt Ratan Tata?

Would he think I'm not keeping up if I didn't say anything? Would it seem arrogant to ask a question in the first meeting on the first day?

But the question I had was genuine, and I really wanted to ask it. Finally, as their pitch came to a close, I bit the bullet and turned to him:

'May I ask something as well, Mr Tata?'

'Of course, go ahead.'

'What stops a new entrant from replicating this exact model? It seems there is almost no barrier to entry, and commercial shipping being cost-sensitive, the industry would probably choose the cheapest competitor.'

Dumb question, dumb question, DUMB QUESTION! I yelled internally the moment the words had left my mouth.

I couldn't tell what Mr Tata thought about the question. He rarely gave readable reactions in meetings, which made guests so very anxious. Man, he would kill at poker. It was a genuine question and I was glad I had asked it, but that didn't mean I didn't care about what he thought. Unfortunately, there was no way of finding out. The answer that followed was not all that satisfactory, and as the rambling trailed off the presentation came to an end.

It wasn't a great concept. And after the awkward mention of how much capital they needed and how grateful they would be to have Mr Tata invest, they left.

'What do you think, Mr Tata?'

'I don't think this is an industry I feel connected to. I have never had much interaction with commercial shipping, nor does it excite me. I won't be able to add value. We can, of course, meet them again next year and see where they've reached.'

And that was that. He had another meeting to go to, but before he did, he oriented me a little bit again.

'There are several start-up proposals sent to us that need to be looked at. Why don't you go through those and give me evaluations on each? You might want to look at the older archives and see what start-ups we have been interested in in the past. See the pattern there.'

It is important to note here the very veiled but calculated effort that he put in to make sure I felt purposed from the very first day, from the moment he stepped into office. These efforts have not just grown with time, but have grown in an organized, directed manner. Very much like an overenthusiastic merman, I dived right into the start-up files.

By the next morning, I had evaluated three different companies, which he looked over during lunch. Silence, spoonful of soup, silence, another spoonful, and more silence as he went through them all. He gave suggestions as to which parameters he would like to see elaborated and which he didn't care for at all. Good feedback and good vibes, until he suddenly went:

'Okay, let me test you.'

He clearly saw my eyes widen all the way up and leave my forehead because the next thing he said was:

'It's okay, don't feel strangled. So, you said the single-engine helicopter still performs as well as a dual engine. Why is that?'

'Well, I believe that the Honeywell HTS900 engine and a very strong focus on reducing weight using composite materials have helped them achieve twin engine performance, and they say their monocoque design aids this, but I don't know exactly how.'

'Correct! You passed.'

The takeaway here was not the fact that he asks questions, but the lesson that he intentionally or otherwise conveyed here: read everything carefully, and then read some more. If one is reading and summarizing a particular document, one should also know the background details for reference, not just surface data. If you have to go back and forth to answer questions, you've not really done a good job, or a complete job. He made me practise this every day. If he has a question, you don't return with just that answer, you come prepared for ten more questions about it.

The volume of start-up pitches that get sent to his office is overwhelming. Everyone wants to get funded by Mr Ratan Tata. If I had to categorize the investment proposals we receive very broadly, they would be as follows:

- People who have an idea, and an idea alone, but not an execution plan.
- People who reach out with miscellaneous concepts in the hope that just the generosity of Mr Tata's office would get them funded.

- Start-ups who launched and failed, but are looking for fund infusions to save the company on its last legs.
- Worthy concepts with a good team and commitment to the idea.
- Companies in which we have already made investments seeking follow-up funding for their subsequent rounds.

It was a lot to wade through. There used to be someone working in Mr Tata's office responding to all of these for a short while. The start-up ecosystem in India, although fast-evolving, is very primitive, especially in terms of who gets access to entrepreneurship. But such rejections did nothing for the ecosystem. Besides, what bothered me the most was the fact that one-line rejections were far from representing who Mr Tata is as a person and what he stands for. The office should reflect his empathy.

I decided to try and not shut out eager hopefuls in this mechanical way. Even when I had to send rejections, my first email would not be a rejection. Most start-ups would not send their concepts in the form of a pitch deck. When I started asking for pitch decks, I either received a haphazard PowerPoint presentation or questions asking me what a pitch deck even was. So I made a small outline of a pitch deck, and made it a point to send it across in the first email. That way even if the proposal was rejected in the second email, the entrepreneur would at least walk away knowing what a pitch deck was. The next time they pitched to a VC, they would not be lost. Even with rejections, I spent time apologizing for not being able to help and wishing them the best in their endeavours. With all this, we never got another negative response or follow-up.

See, to understand this better, I guess the best analogy is a job interview. You give an interview, and then you get told you were rejected. But that's all you know. They don't tell you why. You don't know which parts of yourself to work on. This leaves candidates to assume reasons, which is just cruel. Self-doubt and low self-worth follow.

The only challenge, of course, was the volume of emails. To respond to each one personally, without a mechanical undertone and with the best interest of the start-up in mind, was and still is tough. But it has to be this way. It has to be polite, humane and in the best interest of the receiver. It is, after all, the office of Mr Ratan Tata. However, as the volumes kept growing, I decided to address this outside of the office by putting together an online course of entrepreneurial basics called 'On Your Sparks'. With Mr Tata's blessings, I started delivering these sessions to several students who had the spirit of entrepreneurship but were crippled by not knowing the fundamentals, or what it means to be an entrepreneur, or how to come up with an idea and what pitfalls to avoid. I might have learnt a lot about entrepreneurship at Cornell, but that didn't necessarily mean only Cornellians should have access to some very basic principles of what it means to be an entrepreneur and how to start your journey. That, combined with Mr Tata's teachings at the office, has helped 'On Your Sparks' reach out to and teach almost 300 students a month, eager to apply themselves in the Indian entrepreneurship scene.

As the days went by, I sat in on more and more meetings, but this one time was special. It was a meeting to discuss modular innovative solutions for primary healthcare with the help of a medical school abroad. Once the team made their introductions, Mr Tata introduced me:

'This is my colleague, Shantaa-nu. He has recently joined my office ...' And I don't remember a word after that. He called me a colleague. He could have said assistant. Junior. New hire. A lot of things that didn't put me on such a level. But he said 'colleague', and he has introduced me as one ever since.

As much as his humility is at play in this incident, one has to understand the ripple effects of such gestures in business. The moment you address and treat subordinates as colleagues, there is little room for disagreement, and the subordinates really put in the effort to live up to that treatment. It is a healthy and heartfelt management lesson.

I finished the day smiling. I was a colleague. I could feel myself take a step forward every day towards becoming a comfortable part of his office, understanding what his expectations are, which, honestly, is a tricky process. Imagine working for the man you respect the most, look up to the most, idolized the most your entire childhood. The fear of failing to live up to the role was always peeking over my shoulder.

My business cards had arrived the same day, and, for the first time, I typed my signature at the end of the last email of that day:

Shantanu Naidu,

Office of Mr Ratan N. Tata

13

Pedestal

In my first week at work, Parizaad instructed me to escort Mr Tata downstairs whenever he would leave to go home or, for that matter, wherever he went.

I protested: 'But I'm not sure he would like it. Shouldn't I ask him first?'

'No, just do it. There has to be someone at his side always. Venkat did it, and so should you.'

And so I did. Whenever he left office, I shadowed him. It was mostly when he left office, to walk him to the car and open the door for him, catch up on any pending items on the way down and take down parting instructions, if any. Another primary purpose of the elevator ride down, though, was clearly banter, specifically taunts about aspects of my appearance such as hair or clothing, including but not limited to:

'Stop copying my shirts.'

'Nice bag—for a school kid.'

'You're coming into the next meeting only if you cut your hair.'

The shadowing grew quickly as he asked me to accompany him to more and more places so that we could discuss or work in the car. Many events I would only escort him to, and then wait outside or go back to office to work based on what we had discussed. The boss–assistant relationship was evolving and cementing very quickly. But it felt like it was happening at the cost of our personal friendship. I could no longer see the friend in him speak to me. My fears of one replacing the other were turning out to be ominously true.

Things continued this way. I didn't see him much any more outside of the office. Communications were professional, work-related. The vulnerability had disappeared.

Regardless, every time I felt this, I reminded myself of where my duties lay. They lay now first with the office. I tried to be self-aware of the unique position I was in, to be able to learn from such a colourful and diverse set of responsibilities and a whole bank of experiences that is Mr Tata. I was asked to be a part of more and more meetings. Some of them would be at the Taj, some at the office, some at the World Trade

Center. Shadowing him was sometimes stressful. You had to be aware of the mob that might recognize him and have papers and information ready on demand. Sometimes a few people would ask for pictures and sometimes too many. But he never shooed anyone away.

There was no paraphernalia around his arrival anywhere. No bulky bodyguards or security detail. No entourage. I had raised this concern once but he said, 'Who would want to hurt me?' There were always just one or two people to receive him and escort him to the meeting wherever we went.

Eventually, through sheer repetition of the skinny me trailing behind him everywhere, it was a given that I would accompany Mr Tata wherever he went. When he went through security, he would carry nothing, but I always had the office bag, so I would take longer. And even though I panic, trip, drop things, worrying I will be left behind, he's never gone ahead without me. He always waits, turns around to see me pick up my bag, things I dropped, papers that fell, and lets me run up to him.

When he does get mobbed for pictures, I have never interfered, or said no on his behalf, or pushed someone back, or stopped someone from meeting him. That decision will always and should always rest with him. He is not fond of anyone else responding on his behalf, let alone be rude to a stranger. Even if he has to decline a request, he will let them down gently. The humility that he exhibits is not just for him, it is expected of everyone who is associated with him and accompanies him. But I believe the source of such behaviour can only be true empathy.

The categories and patterns of the meetings I was invited to slowly became clear. They were largely investment-related, but other ones involved innovative breakthroughs, especially in healthcare, or possible social impact collaborations, say between the Trusts and universities or tech companies with exciting ventures, or even update meetings on his electric vehicle venture. I did not make my presence felt. I didn't think it was time yet. I assumed the responsibility of assimilating information and refining it for him in the form

of summarized conclusions, which he could glance over, debate, agree with or act on with me later.

He encouraged discussion. He encouraged contrasting perspectives and devil's advocacy was not at all an issue. But it had to have a healthy motive: arriving at an analytically validated conclusion. If your motive was rooted in prejudice or bias, then the discussion would be pointless, frustrating and unwelcome.

'Mr Tata, I hope I am in my place when I counter something you might have suggested.'

'No, no. I welcome your views, even if they oppose mine, as long as you're doing it for the right reasons.'

Instructions like these were the foundation of my understanding of how I was supposed to deliver my responsibilities. But the spectrum of my responsibilities was ... vast. From registering his new puppies and buying them tick powder, to providing calendar updates, and churning out investment evaluations or updating him on developments related to the Trusts. I loved every bit of it, because it was constantly fluid, no rest stops.

There was a time when he was not particularly in a good mood for quite a few days. Deepthi told me he was looking for an archived letter from 1996 and we couldn't find it. Even in my completely unrelated discussions with him he used to bring it up with great agitation. When Mr Tata wants something dug up, he wants it within a short span of time and, to be honest, there is no reason why he shouldn't get it in that time. But that meant the office was under fire.

'How can I help?'

'Well, if you find this letter, I would put you on a pedestal!'

What a fat, juicy incentive. I had to find it.

Years ago, after he retired as group chairman, all the hard-copy letters and memos were converted into a digital archive. While it worked, some were not scanned due to human error or the sheer physical state of the letter. I ploughed through the digital archives. It was a memo written by him to Russi Mody, a former leading member of the Tata group, in 1996. I cannot reveal its entire contents, but it was important to him and I didn't ask why. It was a memo regarding the controversy surrounding the creation of faux executive positions within the group. After exhaustive screen time I went to Parizaad and finally declared it missing. She told me that we still had the hard copies lying in a warehouse somewhere.

I asked Mr Tata for an approximate timeline of when he had written the memo, and he gave me a rather accurate one.

'I sent it in 1996 in November, just two days before I left for my Christmas holidays.'

I can't even remember what I did on my last birthday. There is no archive more accurate than his memory. And it comes with additional details, the kind which one wouldn't even care to remember.

I called for the files from the warehouse and came to office the next day to find the conference room flooded with musty files full of yellowed pages. The files had completely invaded the office. As I started going through them, one yellowed page at a time, I came across so much history. Some trivial, some important. Some were letters from him wishing everyone happy holidays, some were memos actioning exciting new changes. It was bittersweet, bitter because I wish I had been a part of that era. What a time it would have been to serve him then, when everything must have been a hundred times more alive during his time as chairman of Tata Sons. Sweet because I still get to serve him, a role people would wait their entire lives for.

At the end of that workday, I was down to the last two files with no luck. While I did flag other memos sent to Russi

Mody around that time, they weren't the right ones. I was losing sight of the pedestal. In the last file from '96 I went through the papers pertaining to the time period he had given me. The letter wasn't there. Out of curiosity, and to exhaust all options once and for all, I turned to the letters from just before that month.

'Dear Russi ...'

I speed-read through it, getting up from my chair dramatically as I did. That was it. That was the letter! I showed it to Parizaad and she confirmed it. Someone had misfiled it. I called Mr Tata and told him that I had some papers to hand over, and that I would drop by his place. He asked me if there was an update on the letter. 'No,' I lied through my teeth.

It was a calm evening. We sat in the hall with the blinds open to the sea. But he was shrouded in a grey cloud still. Constant travel and not finding the memo had put him in a rather sour mood. I went through the daily updates with him that were pending. And finally, after everything was done, I handed him the letter. 'A gift, for you ...'

For a solid half-minute, he stared at it trying to figure out the contents, and it was a satisfying moment to see his eyes go wide as he realized what it was.

'YOU FOUND IT!'

'Yes, I did!'

I waited patiently for him to finish reading it.

'I could give you a hug. This makes me feel much less depressed.'

'I'll take that offer, but where is my pedestal?'

'You're so small, we could get a small one and put it in the garden out there.'

'Okay ... if you want a big crowd of girls there,

'...or a bunch of cows...'

The cloud was suddenly lifted off him. We talked for a long time. Talked and laughed. Reminisced about older times, in Mumbai and in New York. He explained why the letter was important.

'All these letters are proofs of significant events throughout my time as chairman. Only I live to tell these stories. After me, without proof, nobody would believe any of it, and sometimes I like to revisit them, to see if there are any lessons I learnt that I can apply today.'

Finding this letter did not require any unique skill which I alone possessed. A certain level of persistence? Sure. But it was more about dragging him out of that grey morose state, seeing him smile again, or ticking one more thing off the 'things that are burdening him' list. Cos him happy is a real joy for the world, no exaggeration.

That evening, I told him that when I write a book, I would write about another side of him and not just historic events or business milestones. I would write about us and our adventures together, and how I saw him, colours and shades of him unknown to the world. Life beyond the great steel wall of 'industry doyen'. Because at the end of the day, the country forgets that he too, laughing, crying or morose, is a human among us all. With moods and emotions, worries and joys.

He agreed. 'There cannot be one book that captures everything. There are different takes, different authors, different perspectives. There may be three, four, five ... So you do your thing, give your perspective.'

After some harmless insult-laced banter and cheeky jokes, I took his leave.

'I'm very happy.'

'I'm happy that you're happy, Mr Tata.'

He patted me on the back and off I went. I hadn't seen my friend properly ever since I had returned to Mumbai, only my boss. The belief that our professional relationship had taken over the personal one had almost set in. But that evening made me believe he was still in there. That fairly ordinary evening is a memory of us being happy, even if for a few moments.

Lighthouses get shrouded too. Sometimes there's fog, sometimes mist, sometimes a storm. But the beacon is always lit. It's always there.

14

Around the World

TRAVEL IS A GIGANTIC part of Mr Tata's work life. Given all the advisory boards, councils and trusts that he is a part of, he goes away for weeks at a time. I don't understand how he switches time zones and flights like he switches outfits, juggles commitments and still shows up at office the very next day after he's back. Whereas a short Delhi–Mumbai flight leaves me feeling spent for an entire day.

But the big problem when he does, in fact, stay overseas for a long time is the resolution of work and important updates back at the office in Mumbai. When he returns, he has to dive straight into the pending things that get piled up. Being the workaholic that he is, he does get through it, but it's a struggle. There was a time when his assistant used to travel with him everywhere he went, as his moving office, so there was no backlog.

I was told time and again that this role of portable office needed to be filled. But I was not going to initiate it. I didn't believe I had the credibility or the authority to suggest such a thing, nor was I taken by international travel. There are, of course, countries to see and places to visit but I thought there will be a time when I'll do it by myself. I did miss him being around the office when he was gone, but I was just supposed to get used to it.

But you can't be someone's assistant and fulfil your responsibilities without travelling with the person you're trying to assist. It started very circumstantially. My first trip was to Hyderabad on his birthday. We flew in the night before for a south Indian wedding the next day. I had requested the hotel to have two cupcakes and a candle ready at midnight. Vitin, one of his good friends and a flight administration manager who flew with him as part of the flight crew, and I were sitting around chatting in his room at 11 p.m. and I could see him getting drowsy. But I had to keep coming up with some pretext or the other to make sure he stayed awake. We played some very badly made sci-fi action movie to pass the time and ridiculed the overacting. But that held us only till 11.45, at which point I gave up.

'Mr Tata, we have a small surprise for you.'

'Oh, really?'

'Well, hang on a few minutes.'

'Come on, just tell me.'

I finally got the cupcakes and he was instantly visibly awkward.

'Please don't sing the birthday song.'

'And spare you the embarrassment? No, my friend. We're singing the song.'

He tried blowing out the candle twice or thrice and it wouldn't go out. He looked to blame someone but who else could he other than me.

'This is that magic candle thing, isn't it?'

It wasn't.

If you're thinking why it wasn't a larger celebration, or a grander fuss, this is exactly how he wants it. Small, discreet, with a few close friends. I wish I could share the exact wholesome feeling when you see Mr Tata smile. You'd want to spend your life seeing it happen again and again.

The next morning at 8, at the time of his wake-up call, I walked over in my Snoopy pyjamas, and waited for him at breakfast.

'Oh, I didn't expect you to be here ... twinkle-toes.'

We sat in silence, shared buttered toast, read the headlines, and then left to get ready. On subsequent trips, that became a bit of a ritual, in those specific pyjamas: 'Good morning, twinkle-toes.'

I just never wanted him to eat by himself, not that he ever had a problem with it.

We spent the rest of the morning doing what I was there to do. Getting through the paperwork, resolving overdue decisions, prioritizing calendars and brief start-up talks. Exactly what the office needed me to do. We continued working in the car all the way to the wedding. Working in the car was always scary for me and extremely easy for him. If I couldn't find something quickly, for some reason I would automatically heat up and the air-conditioning did nothing for me. I never showed it, though. Well, I guess, he knows by now. By the time we reached, I realized we were pretty much done with the work I had brought with me.

At the very high-profile wedding, a huge welcoming party waiting for him whisked him away in a golf cart and I had to follow it by alternating between embarrassing speed walking and running. I kept myself within reachable distance all through but never intruded. If he needed me, all he had to do was look around and I would know I was needed. For example, at the wedding lunch table, someone pitched him an investment in the middle of finishing his fruit plate and he beckoned me to come and take over. Or, when he wanted to know how much time we had until take-off, I'd go give him an update. Or, when someone confused him with too many directions on where to go next, I would try and clarify things. Or, if someone handed him important papers, I had to protect and assimilate them till we got back to Mumbai. But then I would retreat to the background, as if I wasn't there.

Since it was his birthday and it was a very traditional south Indian wedding, they had arranged a small chanting ceremony for his good health and prosperity. He was seated in a chair and surrounded by about fifteen priests, who started a rhythmic chant, showering him with flowers and rice on and off. It was sheer mischievous delight to see him stuck there helplessly because that is his, and every other introvert's, worst nightmare, worse than the birthday song. I had to capture this. I took out my very red phone and captured everything from the safety of the crowd. As I did, his eyes caught the unmistakable red phone, ran along my arm and up to my eyes, and we burst out laughing. I was caught 'red-handed', but I didn't care. His awkwardness was pure gold and needed to be archived for posterity, obviously.

Suddenly, they were done, and it was time to leave. Back he went in his golf cart and back I went running after it. At the entrance the photographers and wedding escorts were clicking away furiously, taking pictures of him doing basically anything, like getting into the car or breathing. I couldn't get in because they were blocking my side of the door. He got into the car, but the car wouldn't leave because I couldn't get in. Nobody thought he was waiting for a bachcha and everyone mistook me to be a part of the wedding party, till someone finally intervened and escorted me into the car. The paparazzi faces had a similar look of befuddlement that I had seen during my days at Cornell: 'Oh, you were waiting on this kid?'

As we rode off to the airport, Mr Tata looked me dead in the eye and said: 'If anything you recorded sees the light of day, you will have to answer to me.'

And that was that. All the way to the flight, I was removing rice grains from his hair. No matter how many I removed, it was almost as if they kept reappearing. The amount of rice we extracted from his hair that day could feed a family of four. Such was the delightful spectrum of my responsibilities.

On the plane, we tried to complete some residual work, but every time I tried to get some work papers out, he would warn me with raised bushy eyebrows: 'Put that back or this will be your last trip.' My obsession with getting stuff done annoyed him but he was also giving me a very important hint for the future—which he had to say out loud because I was too thick-headed.

'Shantaa-nu, there will be times when we can get through stuff, and there will be times when we can't. And when we can't, don't feel so caught up in getting it done no matter what. It's okay.'

This was hard for me to follow, but I've learnt to practise it somewhat today. Whenever he takes me anywhere, I feel like I must work every waking moment. But what I defined as 'work' was too crude. Work involved arbitrary conversations, it involved him doing nothing too, or just being and listening to his stories, or talking about what we saw outside the aeroplane window. If I let him do all this at the right times, he would let me pull out the 'work' the other times.

Such trips became frequent. Delhi, Bengaluru, Hyderabad, Kolkata. I only went when I was asked to, and when I could contribute and when he was going to have enough time on the trip to work. Never just because. I think the pulling of my leg was his added favourite, and, in all honesty, it was my favourite too because it made him smile.

There came a time when he was leaving on an international trip. He would be gone for three weeks, and the work that would pile up would be quite something. I put a note on his desk asking him if he would need me on this trip too. He returned it to me; it said yes. Little did I know the great test of endurance and patience that lay ahead of me.

With great excitement, I bought a total of two shirts, pressed my only two suits, bought a dignified suitcase he wouldn't be embarrassed by, and counted down the days.

The trip was Ithaca–San Francisco–Los Angeles–Paris.

We were going to Cornell! It was the reunion of the Class of 1959, Mr Tata's batch. Sadly we would be there only for a day, but CORNELL! I never thought I would be returning so soon, and that too with such great company.

The usually big piles of paperwork to take on the trip were bigger, backed and bundled with copious instructions. All the upholstery in the plane was so white that I was worried I would ruin it just by sitting on it. While he spoke to the flight crew in aircraft lingo, I slowly set up my mini office. He humoured me, and we worked a little bit, but before long he fell asleep, and then so did I. I was startled awake later when I felt someone passing me by—it was Mr Tata. He messed up my hair a little bit, signalling we could get back to work.

The views from the window were so diverse. Sometimes mountain ranges with snow, sometimes widespread deserts, sometimes lush hills. A feeling of thankfulness for where I was and who I was with grew warmly. As the hills got greener and the houses closer, it was obvious that Ithaca was approaching.

It was a gorgeous summer day. Clean, deep-blue skies, gentle sunlight, the smell of happy trees and the cosiness of the tucked-away town of Ithaca. In the car, while Mr Tata spoke to our reunion host who had come to pick us up, I was glued to the window, my nose pressed against it, reliving the memories of every avenue and every street and every building, but unable to scream out of joy since my job was dear to me.

The day was going to pass us by rather quickly. Mr Tata is on the Cornell Board of Trustees, which meant that in another two hours we were going to be whisked away to back-to-back meetings, before we actually went to the big reunion dinner at night. The most important meeting was with the Cornell vet school to discuss the hospital in Mumbai. I got only two hours to relive Cornell, meet the professors, take a bath and get ready for the meetings. But I did it all anyway.

It was golden hour, around 6 p.m. The beautiful green quadrangle was lit with the last of the summer rays. Libe Slope was straight out of a dream sequence. I remembered the time I had spent under those endless trees, running around with Winter until the sun went down. We walked past the gorgeous Hogwarts-like castles till we finally arrived at Klarman Hall. A crowd of sixty- to ninety-year-old happy faces constituting the Class of 1959 waited on the footsteps.

'Should I leave you here?'

'No, no. In fact, please come with me. I really don't remember anyone.'

We found a spot to sit and waited. One by one, his classmates recognized who he was, and came up to him.

'Mr Tata, do you remember me?'

'Ratan, I have been waiting to run into you ...'

'You are the most famous of us all ...'

'We are all so proud of you ...'

'I have been following your journey, Ratan ...'

'Please meet my wife ...'

One by one people came up, and finally he started mixing. After some warm moments of laughter and hugs, he returned to our spot on the steps and sat next to me. The photographer was roaming about taking pictures, and she took one of us right there in that moment. A happy picture, the Class of 1959 and Class of 2018 together, sitting in the sun on the steps of Cornell. That, I remember, was one of the most mushy moments of our time together, with not much of a care in the world. We were insulated from everything that was bad. Just two graduates enjoying the sunset in summertime Ithaca.

After all the alumni had posed for the group picture, with him awkwardly, but expectedly, way in the back, barely even to be seen, it was time to go in for dinner. I accompanied him, and as I held the door open for him, there were so many others behind him. Some with a walking stick, some in a wheelchair, some needing a really long time to get in, and I was pleasantly stuck holding the door open for them all.

As I saw those kind, loving, warm, wrinkled faces enter, I wanted to be of help to all of them in any possible way. They radiated such affection, sweetness and gratitude in their temperament. Before entering, each one paused because they had a question for me.

'Are you his son?'

'Are you his nephew?'

'Are you an organizer?'

'When do you graduate?'

'How long have you been holding that door open?'

Honestly, that generation is so kind in its ways and full of stories and wisdom and gratefulness. When I finally got to enter the hall, which by then was as full as could be, we found a quiet table behind a pillar. People could barely see us.

'Don't you want to join them?'

'No, I really don't know anybody. Plus, I don't want to leave you alone.'

At this point, a really sweet old lady from his class, whom I had held the door open for earlier and who had been staring at us and whispering something to the other sweet ladies and their husbands around their table for the longest time, came over.

'Mr Tata ... Ratan, we would like for you and your friend here to please join our table.'

After much back and forth and awkward no-nos, Mr Tata finally gave in and we joined a really long table with the most welcoming faces on both sides. The room was lively and full of chatter and music, and soon enough Mr Tata was immersed in cheerful conversation with his table neighbours. And soon enough, I was immersed in it too. It was a delight to see their dramatic responses when I told them the story of how I ended up where I was.

They talked about their golden days, and stories of how various couples at the table first met. When the food was served, it was too much to ask them to get up from their chairs and walk to the buffet table. I made short runs every time a plate needed to be filled, or if a walking stick fell far from someone's chair, or if the cutlery was missing. It was basic manners, but the gratitude on their faces when you did something so simple was a selfish reward. If I missed something, Mr Tata through sheer eye contact signalled me to go help. This is the type of eye contact that comes naturally to Indian parents. It has the power to silence misbehaviour instantly, or to give oddly specific instructions. This raising of eyebrows and pointing with the eyes went on throughout the night as I kept making short runs. And before we knew it, the night was over.

We put on our coats and walked back down College Avenue, with stomachs full, and hearts fuller. It had been a beautiful night. To be in the place where I had so many memories, where he had so many memories, and now where

we had made some new ones together, felt like our worlds colliding in the rightest way possible.

'They liked you very much. I thought you were very hospitable and homely. Good job, Shantaa-nu.'

'Well, thank you, Mr Tata. And thank you for taking me with you. I had a lovely time.'

'I did too, my friend. Thank you for joining me.'

I lay in bed, looking at the picture the photographer took, thinking of all the kind souls I met, but thinking a lot more about the number of times I saw him smile that day. Ithaca has given me a lot of things that changed my life. It gave me Winter. It gave me lessons I recount painfully. It gave me most of what I know about entrepreneurship. It gave me stories like no other. And now I had another something to add to the already brimming chest of memories you cling on to till the very end.

15

Darling, Je Vous Aime Beaucoup

After our short stay in Ithaca, we moved on to San Francisco, the city of slopes. On the first day I nearly died on the unnecessary morning run. But when I turned around at the top, I could see the Golden Gate slowly emerge from the fog. If only I had enough breath for it to be taken away. But that pretty much was the last nice thing I remember about San Francisco.

As the trip progressed and we spent more time working, Mr Tata got sterner. The gentle connection we had during the evening in Ithaca seemed far behind us. We worked hard when we could, setting aside dedicated time in the hotel, on the flights and in the car. But I was purely in clumsy-assistant mode. Mistakes were highlighted and his words were strong. But reminders are necessary that I work for a boss, not a friend. I took the punches and rallied on the best I could.

On the second day, something went very wrong with my left eye. It was as if there was a foggy filter on it, and it wouldn't go away. I was in his room, half blind, but ignored for the most part, until something work-related came up. And the work was far from perfect. I can't say I wasn't at fault, but this was the first time I was exposed to this stern side. In the office you are together for the work hours. There's a breather till the next workday starts. During travel, however, it was breakfast to dinner. Which meant it couldn't be all sweet, and you couldn't escape mistakes. I'm not complaining. I was learning the intricacies of what perfect work really meant for him. It was the soldier level. And at the soldier level, you can't not get shot.

'You're putting signature requests in front of me but what does it mean?'

'You're goofing up the dates again.'

'You know this or you think you know this?'

He did do the regular shirt, pet toys and upholstery shopping in breaks. During the pet-store ritual, I looked around for soft toys for Winter, like I always do, half-blindly navigating my way till I found one on the shelf. It seemed like the last one. Half engrossed in worry about this new side of Mr Tata, and only being able to half see with my foggy eye, I stood behind him in queue quietly with the soft toy in my hand, until we reached the counter and the lady asked me:

'Umm, sir, do you want that harness?'

'What harness?'

'Sir, that is a display dog. Only the harness on him is for sale.'

I had walked around the entire store with a display dog, half-blind. With great shame I walked back slowly and put it on the shelf. I couldn't catch a break. This was very representative of the new phase of my nervous mistakes under newfound pressure.

We moved on to LA for a day and worked on the flight. He only had one important meeting to go to there. I took those couple of hours to go to all the places that I had visited with Sukrut when I was interning as an assistant cameraman in Hollywood (a story for another time). We would have a maximum of fifty dollars combined, but would take multiple buses, eat five-dollar tacos and buy non-alcoholic beer to get to a beach to sit and do nothing but stare at the Pacific blue. Rodeo Drive, Santa Monica Pier, the road to Burbank—I saw them all in a couple of hours while he wrapped up his meeting. But it's not good to rush nostalgia, just like you shouldn't chug wine.

As we moved from LA to Boston, my vision slowly reappeared but his warmth disappeared even more. I was worried. What stung more was that everyone else had full immunity from his stern side. As we wounded up Boston, there was a sudden change in plan. We were supposed to head straight to the Paris Air Show, but Mr Tata wanted to take a two-day detour to London. I didn't have a British visa. He suggested that I fly to Paris and wait for him there. He would join me for the scheduled work events in two days.

In a way I welcomed this change. The constant internal turmoil of figuring out whether his sternness was personal or professional was taking a toll on me. I looked forward to this two-day reprieve. I did not want to add to the cost of the trip by staying at a hotel and reached out to a friend's sister, Rachit. She was generous enough to let me stay with her. Clumsy—generally but also with excitement—at the Paris immigration counter, I fumbled around for the right papers. I couldn't find them till the very end and eventually the immigration officer gave up and said politely, 'It's fine, just go.' When immigration doesn't trouble you, it is a truly warm welcome. I liked Paris already.

I was put up in her house on the outskirts of the city. The weather was the right kind of sunny—just the way Parisians love it. The sky was clean, the houses worth romanticizing over and cosy. Rachit was away but had been kind enough to set up the room with snacks and everything I could possibly need. But I was too excited to eat. Paris was waiting, and I barely had a full day.

I started walking from the Arc De Triomphe, a beautiful, humongous gateway with a busy traffic circle around it. Clustered policemen on motorbikes were parked at one side. Dancers on the sidewalk, tourists constantly orbiting. There are so many beautiful motorcycles in Paris: classic BMWs and Benellis that you would never find in this time and age. Everyone was dressed chicly and everyone looked like they came off a runway. The scarves, the heels, the wine-coloured shades and the ambitious body frames. That's it, all of Paris is a fashion show!

But the spirit of the city was infectious, electric. I had only experienced it in New York and Mumbai. The sun was out and the people were in their balconies. Narrow lanes were lined with tiny cars. Couples in the windows, groups in cafés and picnics in the park. The city reeked of wine and happiness. Everything that has been said and written about Paris is true, after all. I had imagined the poems to be exaggerated, but no. Every verse was true.

In the brief moments before leaving Boston, Mr Tata had asked me what I was planning to do. I had told him about seeing a friend.

'Are you going to go across Paris falling in love?' he teased.

Till the time I left he hummed this old, melodious French song to taunt me about my hypothetical affairs in Paris. The hum turned to words and then to a clear song through the course of the day. When it was time for me to leave for Paris, he sat me down and on a piece of paper scribbled the words:

Darling, je vous aime beaucoup
Je ne sais pas what to do

'This is what I remember. Hope you can find the song.'

And so I did. It was 'Darling, je vous aime beaucoup' by Nat King Cole. Throughout my time in Paris, I played the track in the background. And I was in love without anyone being there with me, in love with the streets with no place to walk, where you just kind of get whisked away somewhere and before you know it you are in another gorgeous part of the city, which is literally every part.

From the Arc De Triomphe, I walked along the Champs-Élysées, with perfume in the air, rife with art and luxury. I could afford nothing more than a few paintings from the street and a raincoat for Amma, but I went into as many shops as I could, listening to conversations, touching fabric, trying on perfumes and making excuses to reject expensive ties I didn't intend to buy.

As I hung my feet over the sidewalk by the river Seine, Rachit eventually met up with me and that was the beginning of another adventure that involved crepe cafes and wine tastings and making new friends and matchbox Paris apartments. Everyone I met was hustling in the big city, struggling to make it, just like in New York. Their apartments

were so tiny, you would turn around and they would finish. We walked the streets till late in the night, roaming around aimlessly, deciding to go home but not following through. I did dance with the Eiffel a couple of times. The first night we went all the way up at midnight when the twinkling white lights come on for a few minutes.

The other time was on a boat on the Seine. I was glued to the deck the entire time as the Eiffel came closer slowly, and then went far back again as the sun set on us. It was a beautiful two days. My heart was full with love for the city and, naively, I too, with those around me, flirted with the idea of ending up here some day for a more permanent time.

There was one promise I had made to myself, and to Mr Tata. To visit J.R.D. Tata's grave in Paris. Rachit agreed to come with me to the Père Lachaise Cemetery, where he is buried. The final morning, we went through rows and rows of beautiful blossoming gardens and ornate mausoleums to look for JRD's grave.

'Division 89, line 1, first tomb on the left.'

That's all I knew. After forty-five minutes of roaming about and miscommunicated directions, we finally arrived. There were three graves with the Parsi phrase 'Humata Huxta Huvarshta' (good thought, good word, good act) inscribed on them. Rachit gave me a few minutes alone.

I didn't know what to say.

'Your friend is giving me a hard time right now, but you know I care for him deeply. I will do my very best to be there for him, in friendship and in everything else. I wish I knew you too when you were around. I wish I saw you two together. He misses you, it's obvious. But I am blessed to have come upon his life. And I only wish that you watch over him. I will also try, just as he watches over me.'

Yes, it's too mushy, but for anyone who knows even a bit about the nature of Jeh and Mr Tata's relationship, to stand

in front of that grave in the beautiful Père Lachaise Cemetery was a moment of great power and emotion. I set down the purple bouquet, let out a big sigh, and off we went.

Mr Tata was coming in at noon and I got to the hotel a couple of hours before him to set up his schedule for the day, get through the pending papers and look over the itinerary for the Paris Air Show, where he had a dozen work meetings. I was looking forward to his return—I thought I could start afresh. When his car finally pulled in, I rushed to the door.

'Hi, Mr Tata,' I said in my brightest voice, which could have been nauseating to a hungover person, or someone who just got off a long flight. Unfortunately, it wasn't exactly met with the same energy. But I was now more resilient. There were several updates to be taken care of, and we dived right into the work.

The next two days at the Paris Air Show were saturated with learning. In one of the only two suits I had, which I had to protect with my life, we had meetings with all the big guns of aviation. Boeing, Lockheed Martin, Airbus, Gulfstream, Dassault. All the meetings were rushed. All the meetings were full. I was always standing indiscreetly in a corner behind him, noticed by nobody and copiously taking notes. Sometimes the meeting would go on for an hour or more and I would question, very strongly, my decision to stand. But it was either that or not being in the meetings at all. Parizaad had instructed me sternly: 'Be where he is and document everything. He will need it when he gets back and discusses with you. That is why you are going!'

Between meetings, when the pilots would fly the fighter jets, there would be an excited glint in Mr Tata's eyes and we would try to get him to the nearest chalet deck to see the fighters manoeuvring. It was always a paternal moment when he stood next to me and explained what was happening and why it was happening. Those fleeting moments between meetings were probably why he looked forward to the air shows. Even the one we attended in Bengaluru was all about scurrying from viewpoint to viewpoint to catch the action in the air. Only, in India, I have to double up as an unconvincing bodyguard as he would likely get mobbed. In Paris, not so much.

At the end of each day, in the car ride back, I would get quizzed.

'What did you think about aircraft A versus aircraft B?'

'What are the cloud trails behind a flying aeroplane called?'

'Based on that particular cloud trail (pointing at one), can you tell me which direction the aircraft was flying in?'

My viva days were coming back to haunt me. I managed to answer correctly almost every time, but the stress of coming up with the correct answer in a non-existent time window gave me hot flashes. He asked if I was enjoying the test.

'I just want the car ride to end, Mr Tata.'

On the last night of our tour, at dinner, Mr Tata and I went through the upcoming calendar. He wanted to know the date of a particular event and I didn't have it on me. It felt like he really needed it, so I called Parizaad. She had mentioned she would be up till midnight if I needed anything. It was 11 p.m. in India. I called her, got the date, and conveyed it to Mr Tata. But he was far from okay with what I had just done.

'Shantaa-nu, why would you call her now? It's so late! You are never supposed to call and disturb anyone after 9.30 p.m. for work. You should not have done that.'

I made a feeble attempt to explain my arrangement with her but it did not work. One of the most stern outbursts I had faced on the trip, that was my breaking point. I excused myself to go to the washroom, and let it out. I could feel the impostor syndrome creep in. All the resilience built throughout the trip crumbled for a bit. I started questioning if I was in fact fit to work for him? I stared at the mirror and reminded myself: I work for him first and only then is he a friend. And this trip was all about the former. I went out and finished my dinner.

'I'm sorry, Mr Tata. I will remember not to call anyone after 9.30 p.m.' And I followed that religiously.

In hindsight, these outbursts were lessons in disguise. Cumulatively, they were the orientation I was looking for. Moulding doesn't happen with cotton and wool. It happens with heat and hammer. It happens with confrontation, criticism and uncomfortable conversations. This trip had given me clear ideas of what lay ahead in my professional career with him. What was required, how resilient I would

have to be, how thick-skinned to outbursts, and how I could use these to learn and move forward.

We finished the dinner in silence and returned to our rooms. The trip was over. It was time to go home.

On our way to the airport the next day, I mostly kept to myself, until he asked:

'Did you listen to the song I gave you?'

'I did. I played it all over Paris.'

'Well, I could give you another one.'

The city passed us by slowly and, all the way to the airport, he kept giving me song after song after song. Before I was even halfway through one, he would get all excited and say, 'Another one?'

We didn't work much on the way back. It had been enough through the trip. I had also noticed that he needs some time to be by himself, talk about flights and small incidents and trip anecdotes, and you can't push for work in the middle of that.

We got to Mumbai, all burnt out—at least I was. Like I mentioned before, he makes trips of this length at least five times a year, and then comes to work the very next day. I just needed my bed. Two days later he invited me over for dinner. I had grown so accustomed to his trip persona that I had forgotten how he was originally. We sat talking while the dinner got ready.

'I'm sorry I was hard on you. I hope you take it in the right way. I hope you don't mind me pulling your leg. It's only out of affection, and I would expect you to treat me the same way. You have to see that this is a training of sorts. I'm only preparing you.'

He didn't say what he was preparing me for. Life? Working with him? The world? I would like to believe it's all of those. For the first time since Ithaca I could feel something other than stressed. But then, at that untimely—or rather timely—moment, I remembered what Deepthi had once told me, which I had forgotten through the trip.

'The day he gets mad at you and shows it, know that you have truly been accepted into this office.'

And so it was. With a full stomach and a fuller heart, I walked home, knowing that my friend and my boss were both where they were supposed to be. Knowing that it was the beginning of a very steep learning curve. Knowing that doubts and difficulties were going to be tests of faith, in myself and in him.

Knowing that I was now accepted into the office of the chairman.

16

Lily

I KNEW TATA MOTORS was winding up the Tata Nano production. I had promised Amma I would get her one some day. But it seemed that the days had run out.

Naina was replacing the family car with another Tata car, and while we were at the showroom to have it delivered, I saw a white Nano parked outside.

'Are they still making these?'

'No, sir, they've stopped production.'

'So which is this one?'

'It's the last one we had, and there are two left in the factory.'

I didn't say or do anything. We went home in our new family car, which wasn't a Nano, but still a big deal for the family.

The thing about mothers is you would imagine they can't read you because you went around the world and changed as an adult and found independence, but there is no greater lie. They can. And she did. She saw that spark of thought planted in my mind, making me uneasy as it grew.

'You should get it. I know you want it.'

On my way back to Mumbai, I recollected how young I was when the Nano had launched. I was in high school. Kids were mean. Everyone knew my father worked for Tata, and I was in the worst phase of getting bullied at school. From the day the car was launched my pet name became 'Nano'. This was not in a cute-funny way but was meant as an insult.

When I went to Cornell, the Nano was a case study. In fact, it is a case study in most business schools. A case of 'marketing failure'. Yes, yes, everyone believes themselves to be very learned when they talk about the failure of the Nano because it was called the common man's car. The aspirational, status-conscious common man in India never wants what's good for him. He wants what's above him, what he can't reach.

Four people on a motorcycle in the rain—that was the birth of the Nano. A heart that I have come to see so full of empathy wanted this group of people, who risked their lives every day, to just be safe. The community, however, rejected this gesture.

The community believed they were better than it. They believed that the 'common man' tag was an insult. Blame the marketing failure as much as you want, but what pains me is a fact that few talk about: the people killed the Nano.

The very people whose safety was a concern decided to turn their back on it, humiliate it, ignore it. We Indians have

that trait very strongly embedded in us. I do not know what it is a product of, and I will not be analysing our psyche at this point. But when something good is born in the country, the first reaction is to strip it, humiliate it, spot flaws, create a narrative, and the favourite: state why it wouldn't work. It is rarely supported or nurtured, it is never respected for the attempt. But, most crucially, all this is never based on complete knowledge, only controversial hearsay. I went through this with Motopaws. Every entrepreneur I know has been through this. I can't imagine what Mr Tata must have gone through with the Nano. The chance to earn public support was snatched away because it was called the people's car. All because of that tag, it never even got to the households it was supposed to reach. There was nothing wrong with the product, so it deserved a chance and then a judgement, but it was never given the opportunity—all because of a petty, classist reason. But this 'product' wasn't just a product. Its true purpose was the safety of rural and sub-urban families that often risked lives with multiple passengers riding on two-wheelers. That effort was trumped by hollow trolling: a product of the aspirational mindset of Indian buyers and not the car itself.

But that was the problem, wasn't it? It was treated as his project. His baby. Not the people's. Nobody wanted to treat it as a step for the collective good. Even before the Nano was launched, there were people standing by to kill it. There was no marvel and wonder around the purpose of that vehicle. There was ridicule.

I remember defending this point to death in marketing class. Of course, I was the only one. Not even the other Indians wanted to say anything about it, other than the usual narrative of 'marketing blunder'.

On a flight with Mr Tata, I finally asked him:

'Mr Tata, I think I'm going to buy a Nano. Winter now lives with me and I'd love to take him places. Plus the monsoons are coming. What do you think?'

His eyes lit up. I'd like to believe that was how they lit up when he helped create it.

'That would be very nice. You should go for it.'

He then went on to enquire about the model, transmission, colour. And as I saw him ask questions and talk about it, I realized why I *really* wanted the Nano.

I wanted to hold on to this part of him. The world could crumble around the Nano if it wanted to. But I wanted to preserve this piece of him and show him that, if nobody else, I believed. That I always had. That he was right and that the world was indifferent to his empathy. But instead of saying all this, I decided to actually do it: bring home the Nano.

I called the showroom in Pune again. There weren't two Nanos left at the plant any more, there was only one. I told them to book it. I had no choice of colour, model or transmission. It was the only one left. A pearl-ish white Nano XTA automatic. It was a memorable day to go collect her from the showroom. Celebrating her arrival with a pooja thali, coconut and garland—a wholesome tradition of marking new beginnings—we were in love with her since we saw her. A cute, amicable car. The space inside was not 'nano'-sized in any sense. With a high ceiling, and astoundingly plenty room for the driver plus four passengers, I knew I had made the right decision. The transmission was smooth, the windshield huge and open with minimal interference, and the way one could manoeuvre it through lanes and alleys was such joy. If you're thinking this is a plug for the Nano, it can't be, since they don't even make them any more.

Looking at its beautiful single-curved outline made me happy. A cute town car that had my heart. As I saw Naina go all around it, and Amma draw tilaks on it, I realized that, unlike any other car we had owned or would own, this was going to be a family heirloom.

The registration number came out to be MH-12-RT-****. My parents joked about the RT initials, and while I told them they were overdoing it, deep down I felt happy those were the letters. After much discussion we christened her 'Lily'—white, fresh and full of joy.

The moment Lily arrived in Mumbai, I took her straight to Mr Tata. He did the same thing my parents did, only he was a million times cuter. He went around examining every inch of it, opening doors, playing with switches, looking through the window, looking out of the window.

'Such a cute little thing.'

'I agree. I'm very happy with her.'

'That is really heartening, my friend.'

The next few days were amazing. I had seen Mumbai but not like this and not with Winter. Winter, with his gigantic head out the window, and I would cruise in little Lily all along Marine Drive, sometimes to brunch places, sometimes to Bandra, sometimes to make new friends and sometimes

just for the heck of it. He loved the Nano. The moment Lily came into our lives was when Winter's life got much more adventurous. And, believe it or not, failure or not, the Nano still turns heads when we stop at traffic signals, especially when we zoom past bulky SUVs waiting in line. (The sass is intended.) She is cute as a button and everyone pretty much lets her pass. The traffic is much more amicable if you are in a Nano. Every other day I was asked—by the guy at the gas station, or a colleague, or an idle pedestrian, or an older Nano owner—if these were still out there to buy. Sometimes I'd run into another Nano and with a big grin through the window they'd give me a wave or a thumbs-up and Winter and I would return it. Sadly, sweet as the question was, the answer was not.

In 2019, there was a burst of articles all over the media, with one common headline.

'Only one Nano sold in 2019, no more demand'

That didn't make sense. I bought the Nano in 2019, and I already knew for a fact that I was not the only guy who did. Remember the Nano at the showroom? That one got sold too.

In fact, when I was getting mine delivered, two others were visiting the showroom to enquire about buying one. This headline was misinformation.

I reached out to the dealer and informally asked him how many were sold and how many enquiries he had received till that time in 2019. And the numbers definitely didn't say zero or one. The Nanos sold up to July were ten, enquiries 122. That was just one tiny showroom in Pune. Cumulatively, across the country, there are hundreds of showrooms, so why these headlines?

These sales numbers are not exuberant, and yes, clearly the Nano had not done well. But why this unceremonious exit? Why these lies? It hurt to know that killing the Nano wasn't enough, that 'they', the naysayers, didn't even let it exit with dignity. They wouldn't even allow it a respectable farewell. They rushed to shut it down, wipe off its presence from history, bury one of Ratan Tata's most empathetic legacies. And there was nothing I could do about it, nor could he. As a respectable retiree, as much as it would pain him, as much as his heart still had a tiny little room of hope for the Nano, he refused to do anything about it, because he was no longer the chairman nor a part of the group, and he intended to act that way. Painfully ethical.

Today, as those incorrect headlines still show up, and the undignified exit continues, I cling harder on to the Nano. And every person who has owned the car would understand this. Which was also the reason behind something that the showroom in Pune had told me: that half of the people who came looking for the newer models were people who already owned a Nano and wished to upgrade. Sadly, there were none being manufactured.

I had promised Mr Tata I would drive him in my Nano one day. That day arrived in January 2020. He finally found the time to spare. I spent the previous night washing, polishing, waxing, dusting, spraying a cocktail of essential oils, checking to ensure everything was perfect. I even made him a playlist of his favourite songs to listen to in the car.

That winter morning car ride is a happy memory. He whistled with the songs that Lily played, talked about forgotten stories, took in all of Mumbai with a sparkle in his eyes. The man sitting next to me in that cute little button of a car was the man who had contributed in making its very lines and designs. And he was happy. In that moment, Mr Tata and I, with Lily, were meant to be nowhere else—other than to be driving around, whistling our favourite tunes in one of the last Nanos, a fading presence of his strong dream. Perhaps our dignified acknowledgement, or an appropriate farewell for the Nano.

As life with Lily continues, I will say this. If you see Lily on the streets, or any Nano, find the kindness in your heart to remember it as it was meant to be: a symbol of empathy, a gesture to take care not just of a customer but a community. Believe me, my friend, I can testify to this any day you ask me. Until then, there are at least two people who will forever hope that the Nano finds either an unplanned destiny or a dignified goodbye. That much it surely deserves.

17

Banquet

A LOT OF EVENTS, destinies and incidents need to align for a person's path to cross with that of another who will leave a permanent impact on their life. Often, it takes years of wading through an ocean of the wrong people, mining one good person at a time. When Mr Tata entered my life, I thought this was one of those instances, one of those mines. Little did I know that he came with a cluster of the 'right people'. The three ladies at the chairman's office: Parizaad, Deepthi and Denese.

In the early days of my tenure in this office—and when I say early I mean the first couple of weeks—I was reserved, shy and overly polite, and addressed them as 'ma'am'. The three of them today often wish I return to that shy version which, to be honest, has disappeared forever, only to be replaced by something far more mischievous and affectionate. These three are veterans of the office, having spent years with Mr Tata, and so I kept a respectful distance. Every day they would sit around the lunch table, while I would request permission to go downstairs and have lunch with the huge influx of high court lawyers at the lunch houses in the bylanes. Every day I would try and bring them something small, and every day they would offer me something from their tiffin in return.

Parizaad and Deepthi took it upon themselves to mould me properly from day one. Their instructions were clear, strong and unapologetic, the summary of which was this: if your heart and intent are in the right place, mistakes will be forgiven. But when it came to transparency, managing of documents, protection of the inner workings of the office and fundamental ethics, there was no excuse to violate any of it.

Parizaad repeated this often: 'You now represent Mr Tata's office. This means you will now always be seen through that lens. Every move you make, every word you say, every favour you ask for will be a move, word and favour from the office of Mr Ratan Tata. Never abuse the power of this office, never request favours just because you sit here. Your duty is to him and him alone, and that is all that matters.'

She was, after all, the godmother of the office. Nothing sneaked past her. All appointments, requests, mails were vetted by her with a sharp and discerning mind. She had manifested the ethics and morals of Mr Tata, and created an unsaid decorum, one which I came to swear by myself. No person that entered the office got special treatment or was exempt from Parizaad's decorum,

regardless of their stature. For this reason, she is liked by most and disliked by some, but respected by everyone.

Then there was Deepthi. With Deepthi I could be more of myself, in the sense she had a front-row seat to all my mischief and leg pulling. She is more forgiving, more understanding of my whims and misconceptions and has her own way of making me realize how my actions might be right or wrong by letting them take their course. The spectrum of things she has done for me ranges from covering for my work mistakes to changing the dressing on my foot daily when I cut it on a piece of

glass. If Mr Tata wanted a record, a document, a phone call or any information, Deepthi was the operational field 'pixie'.

And then there's Denese at the front desk. The first face you see when you come into the office, and everyone is happy about it. Always polite, always sweet and the closest to my age. Denese quickly turned from a relatable friend to a sister on Raksha Bandhan, and wrestle as we might (quite literally as I cannot escape her choke holds), I know she will come through for me in times of trouble, and she has. The one important role that Denese has already played in this story when I wrote my very first letter to Mr Tata, along with information on Motopaws. That file was bound to fall prey to the mass rejections or mundane acknowledgements issued back then by someone who no longer works there, but Denese did not let that happen. She hung on to the letter, showed it to Deepthi and Parizaad and presented it to Mr Tata when he returned from his travels. That is the sole reason I am where I am today, and even though one might say she simply played her part in this story, I will forever be indebted to her.

After the first few weeks of reserved, formal behaviour, there was a lot of mischief, a lot of pranks, a lot of teaching and a lot of affection that grew a little too fast. In fact, it grew so fast that I feared losing it just as quickly. But I didn't. And

my fears melted away on a particular day when I returned to my desk after lunch and found a witty letter sitting on it: an 'invitation to join the royal lunch table', which was basically the tiniest round table in the corner of the office overlooking Horniman Circle. Those walls have seen breathless laughter and storytelling, and still continue to do so.

TABLE OF THE EXALTED THREE

Dear Shantanu,

This is to inform you that the following resolution was passed at our EGM held on October 1, 2018:

After careful consideration and extensive deliberations, it has been decided that Mr. Shantanu Naidu is hereby permitted to join the lunch table of the Exalted Three with immediate effect so that the vegetarians and non-vegetarians can dine together.

If you accept please report at the Table at 1.00 p.m. sharp with enough food for four.

October 1, 2018

Ladies of The Chairman's Office

It is an honor to have been offered such a prestigious position.

I have dreamt of this day since I was 5. I am simply overwhelmed.

I will make the table proud and will bring food to the table in the hopes that you will try veg once or twice.

I will also "take care" of the mint chocolates.

In the light of this new alliance, taunts will drop by 17%.

Yours hungrily,

While Deepthi, Parizaad and Denese could easily be mistaken as just really good work friends, I realized this connection ran much deeper, and it definitely could not be categorized or put in a bracket. It was just ... just really meaningful, really wholesome. We had each other's backs before our own. If there was a mistake or a goof-up in Mr Tata's work, never has any one of us pointed a finger at one another. In fact, years ago, Mr Tata had commented:

'It is impossible to tell who made the mistake, they never let me find out.'

The nature of the issue that faces any one of us is immaterial, be it family, love, professional, even physical—they have taken care of me as they would of a friend, a son, a nephew.

Most of you reading this already know how truly difficult it is to find a place to work where your colleagues are not constantly competing, bringing you down or orchestrating plots involving your failure that are beyond you. I knew I was truly blessed when I started looking forward to Mondays, hung around even after office hours and meticulously planned the Christmas gifts, hyper-personalized for each one of them.

The support that they offer when I travel with Mr Tata is a relationship similar to that of a satellite and its space station. Wherever I may be with him, if I reach out to them for a detail, a document, information on absolutely anything in the realm of this world, I would receive it, understand it and deliver it to Mr Tata. There was no lag, no shuffling, no waiting. This seamless understanding and the transfer of it holds Mr Tata's office together. Without them, everything collapses. They run this office and guard it with integrity.

The only complaint I might have about this dynamic is that it began too late. I am in constant fear that my time with them is limited, that if I had joined earlier, we would have had much more to share. But that only pushes me to value what I have now, it pushes me to create situations to be with them even more. Like the occasional Sunday cookouts, or shopping after work.

This brings me to what binds us together the strongest: food. The only most critical, important decision that is discussed in a huddle as soon as all of us enter office is what we are having for lunch. It is a balance between our lunchboxes and ordering something for the palate. But whatever is ordered and whatever is on the table is for everyone. Be it neer dosa on Tuesdays or bhajias when it's pouring. There is thorough debate and scouring of menus every morning before planning what to eat. Every day at 1 p.m., Mr Tata has his soup and we have our lunch. If we are with Mr Tata and work goes beyond 1 p.m., it is our grumbling stomachs' eternal responsibility to ask Mr Tata if he wants to have his lunch. The witty responses constitute but are not limited to:

'Oh, so that you can have yours?'

'Of course, you need to have your banquet.'

'Oh, is your banquet ready?'

'Who am I to keep you hungry?'

'I will be done in half the time you will take to finish your huge banquet.'

But he lets us have it. And on days that are busy and saturated with work, we just have to gobble up whatever's there. Even then, the small table is never deprived of laughter and warmth.

The thought of losing this Parsi–Malayali bunch of sweethearts is heart-wrenching. But anyone who is close to Mr Tata has to pass the test of character with these three. Fortunately for me, a young 'un as I came in, they took it upon themselves to make me ready for him. Groomed me to be able to take care of him in every aspect of his life. Shielded me from losing hope when I made a mistake. And while I might have initially thought that their intent was to prepare me for Mr Tata and his office, it looks like they too, like him, have ended up preparing me for life.

I truly must have a lot of good credit from my past birth to have found these women, making me want to be a better person every day. Every thought I have is subconsciously passed through the 'What would these three think?' filter. I can't believe how blessed I am to have a loving family and then another one.

And if they are reading this right now with even half a smile, then the purpose of this chapter has been served. Tiny, strong guardians of the lighthouse: Deepthi, Parizaad, Denese.

18

Sunflower

'WE NEED TO GO get some sun.'

All of October, November and half of December, Mr Tata mentioned only this to me.

'You know, it would be nice to go away for some sun.'

'We should just go. It's nice and sunny.'

We went through some serious fantasy vacation-planning in office for the better part of two months until December arrived, and I could tell it wasn't going to happen. He even joked that if we spent too long together, we probably wouldn't want to see each other's faces when we returned.

'Kerala has tucked-away cottages with a pool. We should go there!'

Mr Tata never takes odd vacations. Historically, the one and only vacation he takes annually is at the year-end, usually starting around Christmas and going on till the first days of the new year. But the past two years had been troubling, and he didn't go. In fact, we were in office on New Year's Eve 2018. But not this time.

It was on the eighteenth of December that we heard of the unfavourable National Company Law Appellate Tribunal (NCLAT) legal development, which was unexpected. I gave him an out and told him it was okay if we did not go if he felt he was not in the right frame of mind to enjoy. But he seemed to want to go even more. He needed to get away.

'I need that swim. And we need that sun.'

On Christmas Eve, we flew to Kovalam, to the Green Cove Resort. He remembered this one cottage with a pool that he had stayed at almost a decade ago, and had requested for the same. If you are wondering, Mr Tata never demands a booking. The world doesn't—and isn't asked to—go topsy-turvy to accommodate him. Whatever dates are available for a particular property are accepted. He would have liked to stay till the new year, but it was not available because of other guests, and he accepted that. As always, there was no use of position or stature. He was just another guest.

The next few days, the manager at the Green Cove treated us with great heart and hospitality. Mr Tata, along with me and Vitin, had only one agenda—that had been chanted in my ears for the past few months:

'Get some sun.'

Our days would begin as lazy sloths till each one of us emerged from our rooms, me in my Christmas pyjamas. At the table the only discussion item was: 'What time should we swim?'

We would return shortly after to the pool. Oh, what a lovely blue pool it was, looking over groves of coconut trees, beyond which was a beautiful sea. You wouldn't know where the sea ended and the sky began. Blossoming trees occasionally dropped a pink flower. Vitin and I would try to find the sunniest spot possible for Mr Tata and lay out his lounge chair there. And after pretty much bathing in sunscreen (Mr Tata has a whole arsenal), we lay down and soaked the sun. There were only three things that made me get up after that:

1. To play a Lee Oscar playlist on the phone, one of his favourite artistes. When 'Before the Rain' played, you could hear a trailing whistle, and you'd turn around to see Mr Tata with arms behind his head, face to the sun, eyes closed and smiling, whistling occasionally to the bits that he remembered.
2. To get pina coladas. My obsession with pina coladas has been historically unhealthy, but it is the official vacation drink wherever you are. Pineapple and coconut! It's an

island in a glass and I swear whoever made this recipe was a happy person. We ordered our non-alcoholic coladas, which I would like to believe now Mr Tata and Vitin are equally addicted to, and participated in the fandom by playing 'Escape' by Rupert Holmes—the pina colada song.

3. To move his lounge chair because the sun kept moving. He was not joking about his love for the sun and was an absolute European about it. If a shadow covered even a part of his face, it was time to move the chair. If his toes caught the shadow, move the chair. Shadow? Move! The! Chair! Vitin and I could barely stay in the sun for longer than an hour and were shamed for not being brave enough to submit to the sun, but he stayed in it for more than half a day. Nobody is happier to see the sun than a sunflower, and Mr Tata clearly was one.

After all of us were baked enough (not that kind), we would enter the pool. By that time there was only one sunny corner left and we would be competing for the prime spot, from where we would ambitiously try to reach for our second round of 'drinks'.

But the shenanigans in the pool revealed a kid-like joy in him that was infectious and not very known. He showed us how to swim end to end while staying underwater, and we boasted of our own swimming achievements.

'I was a gold medallist,' I started.

'In what? Fifty laps in the kiddie pool? I was a varsity swimmer.'

He would then return to the sunshine by the pool. And resume whistling, coupled with napping.

The three of us would then reassemble at the couch, half-drowsy from our own naps, and browse Netflix. The only problem? He had seen everything!

'How about this one?'

'Nice movie, I've seen it.'

'How about this one?'

'Terrible movie! I've definitely seen it.'

'This one?'

'Oh, this is the one where he rescues her but dies himself, isn't it?'

'Well, I don't know, Mr Tata, but thanks for giving the plot away.'

Eventually, this would get so exhausting that we would either end up picking a very good movie or a very, very bad one. Either way, we would watch it till our stomachs rumbled collectively.

I always looked forward to dinner. Less for the food but more for the place where they would set us up. It was a surprise every day. Each night the manager with Vitin's help put us closer to the beach, till on the final one we were right next to the surf. Mr Tata always invited the manager to join the table. Live music played and we would try and guess which song it was, and the breeze would participate without being intrusive. It was a time for him to reminisce and tell us long, old stories from his college or Bombay House days. Everyone at the table would look forward to these animated storytelling sessions every evening. Sometimes, to Vitin's entertainment, he would get on my case, and I would return the favour. Though, at the end of every leg-pulling session, I would still ask, 'Do I still have my job?'

'Sure, you do—till the end of the year.'

The end of the year was four days away.

That was his birthday night. He obviously knew I had planned something with Vitin and the staff. (He called them co-conspirators.)

It was the same as the previous year in Hyderabad. Cupcakes with single candles and a bit of awkward singing and another crappy movie to keep him awake. It was as low-key as possible, and the more low-key it is, the more he appreciates it. Two similar consecutive birthdays later, we now have a pact to celebrate each of his birthdays together, wherever we are.

'Exploring even more beautiful places,' he added with excitement, like a young, slightly buzzed college buddy.

On that night towards the end of our tiny year-end vacation, I could see him in his true element. There was a lot of chaos in his life and a lot of attacks on his legacy, but these moments had shielded him for a few days. The glint in his eye, the cheer and the rumbling Gandalf laugh were the sounds of Ratan Tata being happy. And trust me, it is a privilege to be around him then, because the happiness is ever so contagious.

It is tough to gift something to someone who already has everything. But we traded shirts often, so I gifted him two more, and a memo book to jot down all the things he thinks of at unearthly hours.

On our final morning there, the entire staff gathered for a group picture. The unrealistic disbelief in everyone's eyes at having their picture taken with Ratan Tata made them all radiate with pride and innocent joy. For any Tata employee, it instantly becomes a story to tell for generations. Being the taker of this picture, I had the privilege of looking at all those faces around him, and I could see it—he truly was a sunflower.

I struggle a lot with structuring my thoughts when I have to say something weighty to Mr Tata. And I end up doing the same thing every time: write a letter.

I wrote to him less about our time there and more about the cold reality of the war he was in the middle of. I told him he had weathered storms that were far worse, and he could weather this one too. And I'm sure it barely changes anything he feels when I say things like this, and that for him these might be words of no consequence, but if nothing else, I emphasized again the one thing that might make a dent: that in me he would always have the comfort of a friend.

The world knows him to be a selfless person. But you haven't seen the light and joy in his blessed heart until you have been his friend. And while that might not be possible for all of you reading this, I can only try and make these pages as vivid for you as possible, so you may paint a picture for yourself and see what I see. One day if you come across him, you will remember this version of him too: the sprightly sunflower.

19

Lockdown

BY THE TIME Mr Tata finished reading the manuscript of the book that you're now holding, the Covid-19 pandemic had broken out across the world. As the whole country went into lockdown, I decided to stay back in Mumbai. The Tata Trusts was working from home, and even before Prime Minister Narendra Modi declared a nationwide lockdown, we had discussed shutting down the office and gone ahead and done it. Most of the importance of doing this lay in the fact that Mr Tata is an octogenarian and so at high risk.

As the pandemic revealed its true seriousness and its spread increased, the prime minister declared that the lockdown would go on for a month. And then it was extended by a couple of weeks. And then a couple of weeks more. Nobody was allowed to see Mr Tata. He was in proper isolation from the rest of the world. Nobody except his tentatively one-person office from across the street: me.

With each passing day, as the situation became graver, the true challenges of the pandemic surfaced. Mr Tata became restless each evening that I saw him. His mind and heart were stuck in how the country—and the Trusts—was going to tackle the pandemic. With each passing day that the Trusts was preparing a plan, his restlessness grew, until about the fourth day of the lockdown when, along with his trusted advisors and the new CEO, an attack strategy was formed.

I spent the next several evenings helping identify potential blocks to solidify the strategy. Be it financial, legal, regulatory or data challenges, we went through them one by one, until the time the strategy was ready the way he wanted it. It was sent across the Trusts, and anyone who read it was bound to feel the spark that motivated people to fight the situation collectively.

The whole country was already looking to the Tatas and asking what they were going to do. The whole country was in need of not just the strategy that was drafted, but also in need of hope from a stable, honoured source. A source like the house of Tatas. It was the right time to do a press note as we started executing the strategy. As panic, fear and confusion grew in the country, Mr Tata asked me to draft it.

The note obviously factually talked about committing a sum of Rs 500 crore that the Trusts wasn't going to donate but spend itself on acquiring protective equipment, testing kits and ventilators as well as setting up isolation facilities. But I spent the second half of the note on words that would hopefully give strength to the national spirit. I spoke of the challenges that lay ahead, of the frontline personnel fighting this war, of the long-standing commitment and legacy of the Tatas of rising to any crisis that the country faced. Mr Tata vetted the note in his own manner and, as soon as it was released, it went viral. There was no better time to deploy his online presence. This was his purpose on social media: to be a beacon. Two hours after we put out the note, Tata Sons announced a Rs 1,000-crore commitment. Together, the Tatas had set aside Rs 1,500 crore to fight the pandemic, and even before the commitments were executed, just the announcement itself sent waves of confidence, hope and reassurance across the country.

Mr Tata called to tell me about the note: 'Shantaa-nu, I called to tell you that the note has been received very well. We have a lot of work to do.'

In those weeks, Mr Tata was no longer just my lighthouse, he was everyone's lighthouse.

As the lockdown progressed, a new routine formed itself. Even as we remained in touch on the phone through the day for updates on the Covid-19 strategy, evenings were reserved for me to go over to his place to help him attend to all the pending matters from across the world. We cleared the papers one by one till it was night. It must have been the most one-on-one office time I had with him. Sometimes he would get a sore throat, sometimes I would get the sniffles, but never all the symptoms and we would stop each other from freaking out. I was extra careful because I didn't want to be the one who gave Ratan Tata the coronavirus, nor did I want to bring my friend down. We survived.

In the early part of the lockdown, most of the eateries were closed, and my cook was on leave. Groceries were in short supply. He knew all this and offered me dinner most nights. It would have been unfair to burden his staff, but I did agree every other night when he called me out for lying about having had dinner already. He would even make me small care packages full of snacks and ready-to-eat stuff to take home.

Every time I was about to leave, he would shuffle into the kitchen and come out with one gigantic chewable vitamin-C tablet for me and one for himself, because he strongly believed they helped build immunity. We would then just stare at each other as the never-ending tablet dissolved slowly in our mouths. I have never enjoyed medicine more, only because of the weird confidence it gave him. At a time when I was isolated from my family and Winter was with them in Pune, he rose to fill that emptiness. Despite the troubles of the pandemic, this was the silver lining.

We would browse news channels after dinner and see how the pandemic was raging around the world. In a situation that was clearly going out of control, we would often discuss what had gone wrong, what could be fixed, and what we could do the next morning.

In the middle of the pandemic, there was another set of victims: stray animals dependent on human feeders and restaurants. Because both were under lockdown, the strays were stranded. I had found the one thing to keep me sane through the period. Each morning I soaked kibble, packed it in packets and went around in the Nano looking for hungry streeties. I expected to come across only the friendly stray dogs but, as it turned out, everyone was hungry: crows, squirrels, cats and dogs. Every day I went farther and farther around Town, and people started sending me to areas where they knew the dogs were waiting. And they really were. The most adventurous foray involved going to CST station, deep inside on the main line, to platform number 18, where a whole pack waited, hungry.

Mr Tata could not step out. I let him see the world through my eyes as much as I could. Pictures of the all the cute strays I came across every day were sent to him in the hope that they would make his day. The photos eventually made their way to his sisters, also ardent animal empathizers. When I was faced with shortage of animal food, the two sisters were kind enough to donate more bags throughout the lockdown.

It was an experience one would never have under normal circumstances. To go around the empty lanes of Mumbai and find that the hum

of people's voices had now been replaced with silence and birdsong. The blue of the skies was deeper, the sunshine clearer, the blossoms prettier. It was beautiful and intimidating, a reminder of our insignificance in the larger scheme of the planet.

Over time, I could identify five to six main areas where the animals really needed food and we became friends. The cats would pour out mewing and the dogs would emerge wagging their bushy tails. The crows and birds were always in the background and could recognize the car when it pulled up.

Every evening, I would tell Mr Tata about my morning adventures. He would sit in his chair listening to me wide-eyed. In the grim reality of what lay ahead, we had only these stories. And the large vitamin-C tablets. The only terrible addition was turmeric milk! I detested that concoction, but for the sake of my immunity and his protection, we both had shots of it every evening.

One such evening I told him how I was often stopped at the police checkpoints and would overhear them talk about their plight of standing in the sun for a minimum of twelve-hour shifts without direct access to food or water. It felt wrong to do so much for the strays and not the frontline policemen. I asked Mr Tata if we at the Trusts could do something for them.

'If you can take charge of it, I'd be happy to explore.'

I spent a few days arriving at how many policemen were out on the streets of Mumbai daily, their requirements as per their wards, how much a full hygienic meal would cost, caterers who followed all the norms and how to raise finances. When I finally gave him the proposal, he approved it without the least hesitation. With help from the new CEO, Tata Trusts, well-wishers at Bombay House and the Taj Public Welfare Trust, the daily feeding of policemen on the frontline started. The next day, as I went on my rounds to feed the strays, I saw the hot meal packets being offloaded at the police checkpoints, and I was happy, largely because I worked for someone who didn't hesitate one bit in getting this done. We of course were not alone. I also found the Reliance Foundation covering many wards with meals. The city had come together even in that time of isolation.

The lockdown kept extending and all his meetings became video calls, something he wasn't very accustomed to. I would arrive fifteen minutes before the meeting, set it up for him, prepare the lighting and the right angle, make sure he looked okay, and then he was on his own as I sat by, listening in and taking notes. He insisted I participate in some meetings, some meetings not, and I did as per his directions. These meetings were with universities, incubators, or think tanks asking him to contribute his views about business and entrepreneurship

in the pandemic or projections of what he thought might happen and how institutions should prepare themselves for the future. The meetings turned to webinars, many of which were live and attended in large numbers by the youth of the country. I believe he did a fine job of creating hope where there was none.

Until the lockdown, our interactions had been continuous but not long. Office hours would be full of meetings. There would be long travels. But this was the most constant time we had spent together and, to be honest, through each conversation, as well as through the exposure to the meetings full of rich discussion, I learnt in those few months the most I had since I joined.

I think he thrives the best in crises, be it his own or the country's. As far as connecting with the people was concerned, his recent arrival on some key social media platforms had given him a different, raw and more honest voice, be it in the form of a story from the past, a celebration in the present or a direction for the future. During the lockdown he became a much-adored contributor. It was clearly important to bring him forth on these platforms for the country to be able to see the real person beyond the hard image of an industrial doyen. 'May you be as loved as a Ratan Tata Instagram post' was a common quote going around, which sums up how that went. Some ideas he supported, and some he could not relate to. But it was exciting to release pitch decks, have people ask questions, or dive into his rarely touched archives and bring them to the people to help them learn something new about him outside of what countless interviews had repetitively captured.

The lockdown was an opportunity to give Mr Tata the manuscript of the book that you are now holding in your hands. Like I mentioned earlier, on the day that he finished reading it, he gave me a handwritten letter in his peculiar, cursive handwriting, which, no matter what the words were, always felt extremely personal. The letter was to express how overwhelmed he was reading the short memoir of our journey together so far. But the most special lines were where he also wrote about JRD.

Jeh used to enjoy embarrassing me, but it was our mutual love and affection for each other that grew exponentially. You have many attributes that I admire. You are like a son or younger brother, I enjoy being in your company.

It was his first handwritten letter to me. Who knew all it would take to draw it out of him was to write a book?

That letter will probably be the crown jewel of everything he's done for me. In a timeless box it will stay, along with every picture, note and memory, every curve of the cursive black ink making me happier every time I read it many years from today. I will always keep it safely, to be revisited from time to time, perhaps within the yellowed pages of this very book.

20

I Came Upon a Lighthouse

IT MAY SEEM that after all this time with Mr Tata, people would know about me. They didn't, and that was okay. It was only after a while that someone connected the dots, and in small circles the story of my journey from saving dogs to assisting an industry doyen started to circulate.

One day Humans of Bombay, the blog that collects stories from across the city and puts each up in the form of a short write-up and a heart-warming photo, reached out for an interview. I had never spoken publicly about my association with Mr Tata. And to be honest, I was quite satisfied with the press coverage I had received when Motopaws was launched. But because it was an authentic outlet, and because half-true stories were out there on so many other platforms, I decided I would ask Mr Tata.

I told him how they wanted me to speak about the entire journey and then I completely left it to him to decide if I should accept or reject the interview request. It would be fine either way. Being his shy self, he deserved his right to protect his story and his association if he wished to. But he didn't.

'Of course, go right ahead.'

I confirmed multiple times before I accepted.

After work one day, I met the very young team in Chembur. It was a new feeling to sit down and tell someone how it all began. Up to that point, it had only been Amma and Naina in my audience. But I love telling stories. At the end of my very colourful narration, they asked me:

'Anything else you want to tell us about you or him before we wrap up?'

'No, nothing really. I think that covers it.'

After the photograph I left, but had to run back to tell them one last thing:

'Millennial Dumbledore!'

They stared at me.

'Millennial Dumbledore—that's how I would describe him.'

When the story came out, I expected it to sink in the sea of media content that is floated every minute of every day. It was quite the opposite. It blew up. Like, *blew up*, blew up. Countless people wrote to me about it. People from the Tata Group, the Tata Trusts, people who didn't know me, anyone and everyone who came across it had something to say. At one point, it became so viral that some online tabloids featured the story. It was no longer in my control. Not in anyone's control, really. It had snowballed. Everyone now knew my story, usually posted under one common headline:

'How this 27-year-old got a coveted job with Mr Ratan Tata'

I shouldn't have given away my age like that, especially when I myself am often in denial of it. The spotlight became so intense that my colleagues told me the press was looking for me. I no longer felt comfortable. I felt vulnerable—exposed for the whole world to watch. I felt like at any instant someone would say something truly mean. Though the worst I got was, 'How dare he put his arm around Mr Tata?' referring to the photograph from my reunion night at Cornell.

Even though the meanness never came in its full force, that feeling of constant nakedness was disturbing. I cannot possibly compare myself to an actual celebrity, not even an 'influencer' really. I just had a bit of a unique story is all. But I can tell how horribly difficult life must be for them when their lives are always out there, always scrutinized and criticized. Every time I thought the story had died down, another tabloid picked it up. I went from nobody knowing me to everybody finding out about me almost overnight. The one thing, however, that worried me was what Mr Tata would think about this.

He had seen the interview transcript and approved it, but I wondered if he had come across all the hype. I wrote to him to express how sorry I was if he thought this disrupted his life in any way. A long letter explaining I didn't know how viral this would be. Ten minutes after I sent it, he called me.

'Shantaa-nu, why are you thinking like this? I would never let this affect me and I know this happens. Please don't worry about it.'

His words gave me comfort. I felt brave enough to face the remaining press again and decided to weather it out.

By the time it died down, the story of Ratan Tata's twenty-seven-year-old assistant and how they met because of dogs had appeared almost everywhere in the media. *The Economic Times*, *Business Standard*, pretty much everyone had covered the story in some form or the other. As much as I didn't enjoy this sudden attention, in hindsight it did do one thing: it established an accurate presence. All the scattered fragments of incorrect hearsay about who I was were gone now. There used to be speculative stories, the most amusing one of which was that Mr Tata's security guard's son got into IIT Bombay and that impressed Mr Tata so much that he gave him a job—and that son was me. I have to admit: the internet is a scary place.

If you are wondering, and I wouldn't blame you if you are, whether all this inflated my ego, I think about it a lot too. And the answer would be—I don't think so. And there are two very good reasons for it.

The first, my parents. After every single success or recognition in my life, my mother has constantly reminded me, since my school days, to stay grounded. My parents are pretty self-made. Everything that we have today as a family is the direct result of them starting from scratch. Which is why they understand how fickle success is, and how at the slightest hint of arrogance it will divorce you. Our family has always lived in the fear of good things being taken away from us, because we got them after considerable struggle that I won't get into here, and so we never really experienced the headiness of success in all its glory, and we never even celebrated it. We have always approached that joy with a sense of foreboding.

Which is a shame because sometimes I wish I could celebrate at least for a few moments—experience that joy and pride—but I no longer can. We downplay our successes, pretend as if nothing happened and move on. And to be fair, that has done no harm in my life, except that I have never really been able to be truly happy about milestones.

The other reason, the gentler one, was Mr Tata. Everyone expects me to 'learn his principles', as if they would be intentionally taught to me by him, as if he would sit me down and tell me which values to follow. I thought so too at one time. But what I did not realize was the effect his company has on you, and the best and worst habits are a consequence of this. He never taught me humility. But I will dare say that some of it might have trickled down owing to his constant company every day for most of the day and out of sheer respect and adoration for him. I internalized it subconsciously. Recognition and spotlight lose their sheen when you are around a personality like his for that long. Attention and spotlight begin to seem a bit perverse.

Years have now gone by since I returned from Cornell to Mumbai, and there are habits and routines that have grown to be a part of both of our lives. Weekdays are, of course, for constant work. Not just in the office, but in the car, in other offices, on the phone, in the elevator, whenever my dear workaholic boss needs me. Weekends, however, are for cheeky dinners. Dinners that involve summarizing the week and preparing for the next, or watching a really crappy movie. Sometimes, it is conversations full of reminiscences or thoughts about the future. But they all end in the same way: with paternal hugs and excitement for the week to follow. The goodbye taunts are of the following nature:

'Is that lipstick on your collar? Which shade of Bobby Brown?'

'Off to Starbucks again to try your luck?'

'Which puddle are you going to jump in now?'

Sundays are also for haircuts, often following references to my hair as a pigeon's nest, sparrow's nest, any nest really. Our haircut cycles are now in sufficient sync for both of us to go together. Every time he expects I would cut my hair short enough for him to see my forehead and maybe even grant him a parting line. But every time I disappoint him. I mean I cherish him, but not more than these curls. (Vain, I know.) He has given up now.

'Far be it for me to come between you and your beloved curls,' he says.

One of the lessons that I've learnt at the salon with him is that appreciation should permeate all levels of a workforce.

When he is done with the haircut, he won't just tip the hairdresser, he will tip the person who shampooed his hair, the person who got him coffee, the person who swept the hair off the floor. And then he will turn around to ensure I have done the same, before finally leaving. That's how he teaches me things, in the best way possible: by example. How much you can learn from someone like Ratan Tata is less about him handing out life lessons and more about how attentively you observe and listen.

At the office of Mr Ratan N. Tata, my plate of responsibilities gets fuller and more diverse every day, and I am only grateful for it. Every responsibility creates a new story, a new lesson and gives me a new perspective on who he is and on my own life. I keep my eyes much more open, now that I'm aware of the potential of being in his company, to assimilate learnings that might be subtle but important, that might slip away if I'm too ignorant or dormant. I know what you're thinking. Tell us those lessons, list them, what are the top three things you learnt from Ratan Tata. Unfortunately, there is quite a long way to go before I can write that book. But this book, this book comes from a place of love and heart.

There are many unwritten chapters that lie ahead, a true festival of learning, of looking at challenges in the country he would want to solve, of connecting with the youth that is always eager for even a sentence from him, of friendship and camaraderie, of assisting him in whichever way possible in the afterglow of his legacy, probably creating another one that has more to do with helping communities and less to do with business.

I have seen him survive the infamous legal battle with grace and dignity. I have seen him angry, mad, but rarely sad. I have seen him whistle, and I have seen him play mischief. I have seen him get lost in his own stories, seen his eyes twinkle. I have seen him empathize, look at the skies. I have seen him be there in every important journey I have ventured on, fallen from, or given up on.

How can I not? From no matter how far, the country sees him, bright and strong.

It is not possible to forget the day when I came across this guiding light of a person, shining unapologetically with undiluted affection and empathy for the entire world.

That fated day when I unknowingly entered a tiny piece of history.

That fated day when I came upon a lighthouse.

Acknowledgements

WHEN I MET MR Tata for the first time, Amma gave me a little red diary to write down everything in. She worried that as time went by, my memories of all the meetings with him would become less detailed, fade and might even disappear. Naina encouraged this, of course, and said, 'Some day you will have to tell the world about them.' So yes, let me start with my parents. Without their nudges, this book wouldn't even come into existence.

Then comes Mr Tata, who in no way pulled me back or asked me to change a thing in this endeavour. As much as it was an exercise in vulnerability for me, it was for him too, but he gracefully obliged, and I cannot thank him enough for his trust in me.

Then come the people who *believed* in its existence. My three lovely colleagues—Deepthi, Parizaad and Denese—who egged me on; my illustrator, Sanjana, for bringing it alive with her heart-warming art; my dog Winter, for just being himself and making me believe in the world; and of course the small close circle of friends that caught me falling and helped me stand up straight again. And finally the wonderful team at HarperCollins, especially Siddhesh and Saurav, for putting up with the relentless changes back and forth, and for offering their honest effort to make the book what it is.

I cannot thank you enough.

A Note About the Illustrator

When I was in one of the darkest phases of my life, I met Sanjana through her art. I had given up believing in a lot of different emotions, but Sanjana, with her ever-sweet and empathetic heart, rescued me by giving my stories an ear when nobody else would. It has now been four years that she has listened to and witnessed many of the stories that I have narrated in these pages. And she has always communicated and decorated my words through her illustrations—the true heart of this book—bringing my stories to life and making me believe that they are even worth telling at all. The one thing that I feel—that everyone feels—about her work is that it captures heart, and I think that comes from how pure her own heart is. It is a blessing to have her as a part of this book, of my life. I am sure everyone else who knows her feels that way too. I am sure she has an exciting journey ahead, distributing much-needed grace while illustrating one story at a time.

Thank you, Sanjana.

—Shantanu Naidu

About the Author

FROM COMPOSING MUSIC VIDEOS for social causes during his engineering days, Shantanu Naidu went on to establish himself in animal welfare with his video 'Paws for a cause', which was his entry into the space. During his time as automotive design engineer at Tata Elxsi, he founded a start-up, Motopaws, to put reflective collars on India's stray dogs to prevent night-time road accidents. Mr Ratan Tata became a primary investor in the venture.

After Shantanu's return to India from his MBA at Cornell University in Ithaca, New York, where he spent time diving deep into entrepreneurship, he joined Mr Tata's office as Deputy General Manager, assisting him with day-to-day activities, including philanthropic initiatives, start-up proposals and social media.

During his time at Mr Tata's office, Shantanu found a huge gap in young students' understanding and fear of entrepreneurship and founded 'On Your Sparks', an online entrepreneurship course teaching fundamentals through stories, the proceeds of which are used for animal welfare. He has also founded the 'Cyber Aid Army', which helps victims of cybercrime technologically and through counselling, free of charge.

Shantanu spends most of his time with dogs and engaging students online, coming up with the next best idea or talking about his love for pina coladas and Mumbai.

To know more about the author and illustrator, please visit:

Shantanu Naidu: https://linktr.ee/shantanunaidu

Sanjana Desai: http://linktr.ee/sanjanadesai

Ratan Tata and Shantanu Naidu

Shantanu Naidu presenting a copy of the hardback edition of this book, published in January 2021, to Ratan Tata